MOTHER COUNTRY

Britain's Black Community
on the Home Front
1939–45

STEPHEN BOURNE

The
History
Press

This book is dedicated to Frederick Pease who was killed in an air raid during the London Blitz in February 1941. He is the unknown black civilian 'remembered with honour' and 'commemorated in perpetuity' by the Commonwealth War Graves Commission. According to the Record of Civilian Death (due to war operations), now held in Kensington and Chelsea's local studies archive, Pease was killed in a 'bomb blast' at the age of 60, and had 'no relatives whatsoever'.

First published 2010

The History Press
The Mill, Brimscombe Port
Stroud, Gloucestershire, GL5 2QG
www.thehistorypress.co.uk

© Stephen Bourne, 2010

The right of Stephen Bourne to be identified as the Author
of this work has been asserted in accordance with the
Copyrights, Designs and Patents Act 1988.

British Library Cataloguing in Publication Data.
A catalogue record for this book is available from the British Library.

ISBN 978 0 7524 5610 2

Typesetting and origination by The History Press
Printed in Great Britain
Manufacturing managed by Jellyfish Print Solutions Ltd

CONTENTS

ACKNOWLEDGEMENTS

Arts Council England
Black and Asian Studies Association
BBC Written Archives Centre
British Film Institute
Cuming Museum (London)
Imperial War Museum (London)
Ian Brown
Sean Creighton
Tina Horsley
Keith Howes
Linda Hull
Professor David Killingray
Simon Mason
Marika Sherwood
Aaron Smith
Robert Taylor

The extract from Langston Hughes' *The Man Who Went to War* (see Chapter 9) has been reprinted with the permission of Harold Ober Associates Incorporated (copyright 1944 by Langston Hughes).

Though every care has been taken, if, through inadvertence or failure to trace the present owners, we have included any copyright material without acknowledgement or permission, we offer our apologies to all concerned.

AUTHOR'S NOTE

In *Mother Country* my use of the term 'black' means people of African descent, usually African Americans or Africans, Caribbeans and black Britons. Terms such as 'negro', 'West Indian', 'West Indies' and 'coloured' have been used in their historical contexts, usually before the 1960s and 1970s, the decades in which the term 'black' came into popular use.

This book is not intended to be definitive; the reader will find some gaps. It reflects my interest in the home front, not the military, so there are only a few references to those who served in the armed forces. The experiences of African American GIs have already been extensively covered by Graham Smith in *When Jim Crow Met John Bull – Black American Soldiers in World War II Britain* (I.B. Tauris, 1987) and readers may want to consult the following books for a wider view of the subject: Amos A. Ford's *Telling the Truth – The Life and Times of the British Honduran Forestry Unit in Scotland (1941–44)* (Karia Press, 1985); Marika Sherwood's *Many Struggles – West Indian Workers and Service Personnel in Britain (1939–45)* (Karia Press, 1985); Hakim Adi and Marika Sherwood's *The 1945 Manchester Pan-African Congress Revisited* (New Beacon Books, 1995) and back issues of the newsletters of the Black and Asian Studies Association, founded in 1991.

I wanted to include a chapter about Butetown in Cardiff, which has one of the oldest black communities in Britain, but through no fault of my own I was unable to access the archives of the Butetown History and Arts Centre. However, I have mentioned Butetown in my chapters about women (Chapter 3), evacuees (Chapter 5) and civilian defence (Chapter 6).

INTRODUCTION

'LET US GO FORWARD TOGETHER'

I know too well that we would never allow it to be said of us that when the freedom of the world was at stake we stood aside.

Una Marson (Jamaican broadcaster) in *Calling the West Indies*,
BBC radio broadcast to the West Indies, 3 September 1942

In 2007 I was moved to tears when I attended a memorial to an entire family of thirteen wiped out in the German Blitz on London in 1940. It had taken sixty-seven years for the memorial to be erected. The tragic incident occurred when an underground shelter on Camberwell Green in south-east London took a direct hit from a 500lb German bomb. When I was growing up in London in the 1960s and 1970s, my family told me many stories about life on the home front, which was the name given to the activities of a civilian population in a country at war. I was an impressionable child, and all through my early, formative years, my head was filled with dramatic, true life stories about the Second World War: air raids, evacuation, food shortages, doodlebugs and how communities pulled together and survived these terrible ordeals. I was fascinated by how the war affected my family and everyday people. Unlike other boys, I was not interested in stories about battles on land, sea and air.

The war impacted greatly on my family. In 1940 my mum was evacuated from London to her Irish Catholic grandparents in Merthyr Tydfil, South Wales. She remembered looking over the mountains towards Cardiff on the nights the city was bombed. The sky over Cardiff glowed red, so they knew something terrible was happening, and Granny Murray clutched her rosary beads and prayed.

Thunderstorms reminded my dad of air raids. In the middle of the night, when my sister and I were small children, as soon as a roll of thunder could be heard in the distance, dad would wake us up and carry us downstairs until the storm had passed. We were aware that something terrible had happened to him as a child, but we didn't find out the truth until later. Norman Longmate, a historian of the Second World War, advertised for memories of the doodlebugs (flying bombs) for a book about the subject. Dad wanted to make a contribution to the book and in doing so he revealed to my sister and I the full horror of what had happened to him at the age of 12. In June 1944 a doodlebug exploded and flattened his house (and half his street), and he was caught in the blast. Dad and his family were buried alive. He didn't know how long they remained in the rubble: 'The next thing I can remember was someone picking me up and saying "alright, son. You will be alright now." I was placed on a stretcher at the end of our turning to await the arrival of the ambulance. It was then I realised my face was wet with blood and my eyes would not open.'[1]

Then there was Aunt Esther (see Chapter 4), a black Londoner who became part of my family during the Blitz when my great-grandmother, known as Granny Johnson, 'adopted' her. In their tight-knit working-class community in Fulham, granny was a mother figure, loved and respected by everyone. When Esther's father was killed in 1941, she was left alone. Her only relatives were in British Guiana, so granny offered her a home.

My interest in documenting the experiences of black Londoners on the home front began with the stories my Aunt Esther told me. During the war she gave up her job as a seamstress to do war work. She became a fire watcher during air raids. While recording my aunt's memories, I began searching for other stories of black people in wartime Britain and I discovered many who have been ignored by historians in the hundreds of books and documentaries produced about Britain and the Second World War. For example, when I was still a teenager, I bought a copy of Angus Calder's *The People's War*, first published in 1969. Calder mentioned the existence of a black air-raid warden – E.I. Ekpenyon – in London: 'One Nigerian air raid warden in an inner suburb was regarded as a lucky omen by shelterers.' So at an early age I was made aware that Aunt Esther was not the only black person in London, or indeed Britain, during the war.[2] Some recently published books about Britain and the Second World War have started to acknowledge the black British presence, but not in any depth. In *London at War 1939–1945* Philip Ziegler mentions E.I. Ekpenyon, Learie Constantine and Ken 'Snakehips' Johnson. In *Wartime Britain 1939–1945* Juliet Gardiner also mentions Constantine (though not his war work) and Johnson, and devotes several pages to the plight of the black American GIs, but she doesn't mention Dr Harold Moody and the campaigning work he undertook with his organisation the League of Coloured Peoples. In fact, if historians have acknowledged the black presence in Britain in wartime, it is usually the experiences of black American GIs, not black Britons.

It has been estimated that there were at least 15,000 black and mixed race citizens of African, Caribbean, American and British backgrounds in England, Wales and Scotland when war was declared on 3 September 1939, but the figure could have been as high as 40,000.[3] At the outbreak of war, the largest black communities were to be found in the Butetown (Tiger Bay) area of Cardiff in South Wales, Liverpool and the Canning Town and Custom House area of East London's dockland. In 1935 Nancie Hare's survey of London's black population recorded the presence of 1,500 black seamen and 250–300 working-class families with West Indian or West African heads of households.[4]

Despite evidence of racial discrimination black people contributed to the war effort where they could. In Britain, black people were under fire with the rest of the population in places like Bristol, Cardiff, Liverpool, London and Manchester. Many volunteered as civilian defence workers, such as fire watchers, air-raid wardens, firemen, stretcher-bearers, first-aid workers and mobile canteen personnel. These were activities crucial to the home front, but their roles differed from those in the armed forces. Factory workers, foresters and some nurses were recruited from British colonies in Africa and the West Indies. Before the Second World War, many in Britain viewed the colonies there as backwaters of the British Empire, but when Britain declared war on Germany, the people of the empire immediately rallied behind the 'mother country' and supported the war effort. Throughout the empire black citizens demonstrated their loyalty. Many believed that Britain would give them independence in the post-war years, but they recognised that, for this to happen, a battle had to be won between the 'free world' and fascism. This instilled a sense of duty in many citizens of the empire. Many in the colonies made important contributions, for example, by volunteering to join the armed services, coming to Britain to work in factories, donating money to pay for planes and tanks, and knitting socks and balaclavas. This important input to the war effort has been ignored by historians. For some it may seem strange that black people would support a war alongside white people who did not treat them with equality, but the need to win the war, and avoid Nazi occupation, outweighed this.

In the course of my research, many stories came to light about black servicemen and women, and civilians, facing up to racist attitudes in wartime Britain from both the British and American men who were based there. After the USA entered the war in December 1941, in the following year, the arrival of around 150,000 African American US soldiers added to the moral panic of 'racial mixing'. Black American GIs were segregated from white GIs, but black Britons and their colonial African and West Indian counterparts served in mixed units. It was not uncommon for non-American blacks in Britain to find themselves subjected to racist taunts and violence from visiting white American GIs. Conscious of the abuse some black Britons were being subjected to, in 1942 the Colonial Office recommended that they wear a badge to differentiate them from African Americans. Harold Macmillan MP supported the idea and suggested 'a little Union Jack to wear in their buttonholes'. Needless to say, the idea came to nothing.[5]

One story that sticks in my mind is that of Jack Artis, a black British army sergeant who, before he died in 1998, told stories to younger members of his family about racist attitudes in wartime Britain. Jack particularly loathed the white American GIs. His wife Joan, whom he married in 1944, related a story that illustrates this. There was a family reunion in a local pub, a rare occasion which allowed them all to be together, including several who were serving in the armed forces (two in the army, two in the navy and one in the RAF): 'Into the pub came some white GIs, apparently some snide remarks were not long forthcoming from the GIs, all aimed at Uncle Jack. The GIs got more than they bargained for as the people in the pub (besides our family) all knew and liked Jack. The GIs were turned upon and after a "scuffle" were unceremoniously ejected from the pub and told not to return again in no uncertain terms.' Jack Artis added: 'We were there to fight the Nazis, who believed in white supremacy, so God alone knows what they [the GIs] thought they were fighting for.'[6]

Very little information has been made available about black people and the Second World War. In books about the home front historians and television documentaries perpetuated the myth that only white people took part. In the 1990s the Imperial War Museum, with the help of consultants and experts like Marika Sherwood from the Black and Asian Studies Association, Linda Bellos, a local activist in Lambeth and the historian Ben Bousquet, began to acknowledge the existence of black servicemen and women in wartime. The museum achieved this with exhibitions, talks and 'Together' (1995), a multi-media resource pack aimed at schools, but information about the black presence on the home front was mostly absent. In September 2000 I tried to address this with an article about the subject in *BBC History Magazine*, which was later reprinted in the *Black and Asian Studies Newsletter*. By then I had learned a great deal about the wartime contributions of Dr Harold Moody (see Chapter 1) and Learie Constantine (see Chapter 2), published books about Aunt Esther and the singer Adelaide Hall (see Chapter 7), interviewed a black evacuee from London's East End (see Chapter 5), read E.I. Ekpenyon's *Some Experiences of an African Air Raid Warden* (1943) (see Chapter 6) and Delia Jarrett-Macauley's acclaimed biography of the BBC producer Una Marson (see Chapter 9), began interviewing people from the former colonies in Africa and the West Indies about their experiences of the home front (see Chapter 11), and discovered what might have happened to Aunt Esther and other black people in this country if Hitler had invaded Britain in 1940 (see Postscript).

With lots of interesting material – and hope – I began to approach publishers with a proposal for this book, but I was unprepared for the rejections. On a positive note, the Imperial War Museum invited me to present a talk about the black presence on the home front during Black History Month in 2002, and they continued to do so for several years. In 2008 they invited me to join a group of consultants on their 'War to Windrush' exhibition.

In spite of the success of 'War to Windrush' and a similar exhibition that I helped to research which also looked at black participation in wartime, 'Keep Smiling Through – Black Londoners on the Home Front 1939–1945', at the nearby Cuming Museum, absences still exist. For example, to mark the seventieth anniversary of the outbreak of the Second World War on 3 September 2009, a week-long series of television programmes was shown on BBC1 from 7–11 September; the daytime series *The Week We Went to War*, presented by Katherine Jenkins and Michael Aspel, celebrated the heroes of the home front. However, black people who contributed to the war effort remained unmentioned. The Imperial War Museum's 'Outbreak 1939' exhibition was more inclusive, and made room for the Nigerian air-raid warden E.I. Ekpenyon and the singer Adelaide Hall, who was prominently showcased with her white contemporaries, Gracie Fields and Vera Lynn. 'Outbreak 1939' sent a small flare into the night sky. I hope that *Mother Country* will help to light up that sky and draw attention to a subject that has been neglected for far too long. Thanks to The History Press, this has been made possible.

CHAPTER 1

DR HAROLD MOODY:
BRITAIN'S MARTIN LUTHER KING JR

Dr Harold Moody was born in Jamaica but lived in Peckham, south-east London, for most of his life, from the Edwardian era until his death in 1947. In the 1930s and 1940s Moody was more than just a popular family doctor. He was an ambassador for Britain's black community and an important fig- urehead who – with his organisation the League of Coloured Peoples (LCP) – campaigned to improve the situation for black people in Britain, especially during the Second World War. In 1972 Edward Scobie described Moody in his book *Black Britannia* as a man whose leadership and strength of character won the respect of English people and carried the League through many dif- ficult periods, gaining it the respect and admiration of white and black alike. Scobie adds that Dr Moody's counterpart could be seen in the charismatic African American leader Dr Martin Luther King Jr:

> They were both devout men with an innate love of mankind and the pro- found belief that in the end, good will prevail. To many extremists among the Africans and West Indians in Britain in the thirties, Dr Moody was looked upon as something of an Uncle Tom – much as Black Power supporters and some extremists looked upon Dr King in his last years. This in no way detracts from the good that Dr Moody and the League of Coloured Peoples did for the thousands of blacks living in Britain between the two world wars.[1]

Harold Moody's Early Life

Harold Arundel Moody was born in Kingston, Jamaica, in 1882, the eldest of six children. Harold's father Charles was a successful businessman. He owned a chemist shop, the Union Drugstore, in West Parade, Kingston, the largest town in Jamaica. Although slavery had been abolished in Jamaica in 1834, Harold's mother Christina had been denied an education. As a young girl she entered domestic service with a white family. Nevertheless, Christina was ambitious for her six children and was a very forceful presence in their lives. She provided a loving and secure home for her family and possessed a sense of humour which was infectious. Christina wanted the best education for all her children, and managed to realise her ambition. For example, Harold's brother Ludlow studied at King's College Hospital in London (1913–18), where he won the Huxley Prize for physiology. He later returned to Jamaica to become the government bacteriologist. Ronald Moody, Harold's third brother, studied dentistry at King's College London, practised for a few years, and then became a professional sculptor.

Harold was encouraged to study hard and did well at school. As a young man he became a devout Christian and his faith was the mainspring of his life and activities. When Harold was growing up, Jamaica was part of the British Empire and Harold was raised on the belief that England was the mother country. His colour may have been a factor in his failure to secure a scholarship to further his education, but in spite of this he was determined to have a career in medicine. With his mother's support, Harold sailed to England in 1904, at the age of 21, to study medicine at King's College Hospital, then situated in Lincoln's Inn Fields, and now at Denmark Hill.

In those days white Britons had little exposure to life in other parts of the British Empire and had limited contact with black people. The black population of Britain may not have numbered more than 20,000 by 1914 and they were mainly concentrated in sea ports, such as Cardiff, Liverpool and London's East End.[2] The young Harold was completely unprepared for life in Edwardian London. He found it hard to find a place to live. On his arrival he had visited the Young Men's Christian Association in Tottenham Court Road where he obtained a list of addresses where he might find accommodation. However, at every address he went to the landlord or landlady turned him away. He finally found somewhere to live in a small and dingy attic room in St Paul's Road, Canonbury.

At this time, Harold often encountered British people whose knowledge and understanding of black culture was limited. They were surprised to meet an educated, well-spoken black man who was more British than themselves. Harold did not allow these experiences to deter him from training to become a doctor and making a new life for himself in the mother country.

Having received several academic awards, Harold qualified as a doctor in 1912, but, though he was the most qualified applicant, he was denied a position at King's College Hospital because of open racial discrimination. He also applied for an appointment as one of the medical officers of the Camberwell Board of Guardians. A doctor who was a member of this board stated publicly that Dr Moody had the best qualifications of all the applicants, but because of racial discrimination he was not given the appointment. Of this incident Harold wrote: 'I retreated gracefully and applied myself to the building up of my private practice.'[3]

Work and Family

Forced into self-employment, the new Dr Moody started his own practice in Peckham at 111 King's Road (now King's Grove) in February 1913. In 1922 Harold moved his family to their second Peckham home: a spacious, rambling Victorian house at 164 Queen's Road. A deeply religious man, he felt strongly that God had called him to serve the people of south-east London. In the first week his takings amounted to just £1, but gradually they increased as the people of nearby Peckham and the Old Kent Road grew to know and trust the sympathetic doctor. His daughter Christine said: 'He was a very popular person in Peckham because of his practice. He was a very good doctor and people appreciated this. People came from far and near to see him.'[4] Dr Moody practised in Peckham in the days before Britain had a National Health Service and working-class families faced hardship when they tried to find money to pay doctors for medical treatment. Dr Moody often treated the children of working-class families for no charge.

Harold also found time for a personal life. In 1913 he married Olive Tranter, a kind, affectionate English nurse. Mixed marriages were uncommon in Edwardian England, and some couples faced hostility and discrimination, especially if they had children. Fearing for the young couple, the Moody and Tranter families tried to persuade them not to marry, but from the start of their relationship the couple were devoted to each other. Their wedding took place at Holy Trinity Church in Henley-on-Thames, Oxfordshire. Harold and Olive had six children, all born in Peckham: Christine, Harold, Charles, Joan, Ronald and Garth. Meanwhile, family and work commitments prevented Harold from visiting Jamaica. He returned on only three occasions, in 1912, 1919 and finally in 1946–47.

Founding the League of Coloured Peoples

As well as being a doctor, Harold Moody was driven to be active in his community. As a Christian, he became involved with church affairs as soon as he arrived in Britain. By 1931 he was president of the London Christian Endeavour Federation, and he became involved in the administration and running of the Camberwell Green Congregational Church in Wren Road, where he was a deacon and lay preacher. He often used church pulpits to put across his views of racial tolerance. English dignitaries attended these services, the highlight being the singing of spirituals. Harold's experiences of hardship and racial discrimination also led him to become the founder and president of the League of Coloured Peoples. The organisation became the first effective pressure group in Britain to work on behalf of its black citizens.

The 1920s and 1930s were a difficult period for black people in Britain, especially settlers from Africa and the Caribbean. Cities like Cardiff, Liverpool and London were often highlighted as places where hotels, restaurants and lodging houses refused to accept black people, but racial prejudice was widespread and institutionalised. Like most settlers of African descent, Harold had become frustrated with the racial discrimination he encountered in Britain. He helped many black people who came to him in distress. They told him about the difficulties they faced in trying to find work or somewhere to live. Sometimes Harold would take it upon himself to confront employers and make a powerful plea on behalf of those who were being victimised. Soon, other middle-class black people in Britain joined Harold in his crusade for equal rights, and before long they realised they would be more effective if they formed an organisation. In 1931 the League of Coloured Peoples was born.

The League had four main aims: 'protect the social, educational, economic and political interests of its members; interest members in the welfare of coloured peoples in all parts of the world; improve relations between the races; and co-operate and affiliate with organisations sympathetic to coloured people.' In 1937 a fifth goal was added: 'to render such financial assistance to coloured people in distress as lies within our capacity.'[5]

In the 1930s the League based itself at Harold's home in Queen's Road, Peckham, which became a popular meeting place for black intellectuals. The visitor's book read like a who's who of black historical figures. Visitors included the famous singer and actor Paul Robeson; Trinidadian historian and novelist C.L.R. James; Kwame Nkrumah, who became president of Ghana; Jomo Kenyatta, who became the founding president of the Republic of Kenya; and the Trinidadian cricketer Learie Constantine (see Chapter 2).

Other black people who had made Britain their home supported Dr Moody and the League, including Dr Cecil Belfield Clarke of Barbados,

George Roberts of Trinidad, Samson Morris of Grenada, Robert Adams of British Guiana and Desmond Buckle of Ghana. Also present at the League's first meeting was Stella Thomas who would later become the first female magistrate in West Africa. Dr Moody saw the League primarily as serving a Christian purpose, not a political one. Yet for two decades the League was the most influential organisation campaigning for the civil rights of African and Caribbean people in Britain. Through various campaigns and *The Keys*, a quarterly journal first published in 1933, the League struck many blows against racism in Britain. It was devoted to serving the interests of African and Caribbean students, and campaigned for African and Caribbean settlers to be given better housing and greater access to employment. For thousands of black people in Britain, *The Keys* was the main vehicle for airing their racial grievances. In 1939 the publication of the journal was suspended due to lack of funds. During the war its place was taken by the *News Letter*.[6]

In 1941, in the League's *News Letter*, Arthur Lewis said: 'At the outbreak of this war spokesmen of the British Government made speeches denouncing the vicious racial policies of Nazi Germany and affirming that the British Empire stands for racial equality. It therefore seemed to the League ... that the time had come once more to direct the Government's attention to its own racial policy, and if possible to get these fine speeches crystallised into action.'[7] The height of the League's influence as a pressure group came in 1943 when the organisation held its twelfth annual general meeting in Liverpool. It was attended by over 500 people and one of the talks concerned 'a charter for colonial freedom'. The following year the League drafted 'A Charter for Coloured People' and the text included a demand for self-government for all colonial peoples. It also declared that all racial discrimination in employment, restaurants, hotels and other public places should be made illegal and 'the same economic, educational, legal and political rights shall be enjoyed by all persons, male and female, whatever their colour'. The charter foreshadowed the resolutions of the 1945 Pan-African Congress in Manchester. The League was the forerunner of such organisations as the Race Relations Board (1965–76) and the Commission for Racial Equality (1976–2007).

'Joe' Moody and Racism in the British Army

During the Second World War, five of Dr Moody's six children received army or RAF commissions. Dr Moody's son Ronald served in the Royal Air Force. His daughter Christine and son Harold both qualified as doctors and, after a short period in practice at Peckham, they joined the Royal Army Medical Corps and became captain and major respectively. Moody's youngest son Garth was a pilot-cadet in the Royal Air Force. However, at the start of the war Dr Moody found himself challenging the war office when one of his sons was informed that he could not become an officer in the British army because he was not 'of pure European descent'.

In 1939 Dr Moody's 22-year-old son Charles Arundel, known as 'Joe', qualified for basic training as an officer in the British army. He went to a recruiting office in Whitehall and was interviewed by a captain. Joe recalled in the Channel 4 television documentary *Lest We Forget* (1990): 'The Captain was obviously quite embarrassed with my being there.'[8] After the captain talked to the major, he informed Joe that he could not become an officer because he was not, in spite of being born in England, 'of pure European descent'. The captain then suggested that Joe join the ranks and hopefully be commissioned as an officer at a later date.

When Joe informed his father about his rejection, Dr Moody fought back. Joe said: 'He immediately picked up the telephone and spoke to the Colonial Office and made an appointment with one of the under-secretaries. That started the wheels in motion for getting the Army Act changed which enabled members of the colonies to have commissions in the forces for the duration of the war.'[9] Dr Moody led the campaign to change the law, and joined other members of the League, as well as the International African Service Bureau (IASB) and the West African Students' Union, to lobby the government. Letters to the press and editorials in *The Keys* and the *News Letter*, reinforced by speeches in public and private lobbying by Dr Moody, all made a difference. On 19 October 1939 the Colonial Office issued the following statement: 'British subjects from the colonies and British protected persons in this country, including those who are not of European descent, are now eligible for emergency commissions in His Majesty's Forces.' But Dr Moody remained unsatisfied: 'We are thankful for this,' he said, but 'we do not want it only for the duration of the war. We want it for all time. If the principle is accepted now, surely it must be acceptable all the time.'[10]

Joe Moody was sent to Dunbar in Scotland where he joined an officer-cadet training unit for four months of intense training. Joe said: 'I was a guinea pig, so I had to be very careful and really perform outstandingly. And I didn't get thrown out so they must have thought I could make it.' When he was commissioned Joe was given some advice by his company commander: 'He took me into his office and he told me that I was going to a good regiment and that I would be the first coloured officer to walk into their officers' mess, and there would be dead silence, but I was not to be embarrassed. And he said, "Joe, do your job and when your time comes to shine you will shine." That was great advice.'[11] In 1940 Joe became only the second black officer in the British army when he joined the Queen's Own Royal West Kent Regiment; the first being Walter Tull in 1917.[12]

Dr Moody and the League of Coloured Peoples during the War

During the Second World War, thousands of black workers and military personnel came to Britain from colonies in Africa and the Caribbean to support the war effort and this increased the workload of Dr Moody and the League, but it also gave him and the organisation greater purpose and influence. In 1940 Dr Moody forced the BBC to apologise after a radio announcer used the word 'nigger' during a broadcast. He complained that 'this is one of the unfortunate relics of the days of slavery, vexatious to present day Africans and West Indians, and an evidence of incivility on the part of its user'.[13] In a written statement to Dr Moody, dated 16 May 1940, the BBC admitted liability for the presenter's comments and offered a full apology. In 1942 Dr Moody wrote a letter of protest to the director general of the BBC after the exclusion of Africans and West Indians from their radio programme *Good Night to the Forces*.

When the Jamaican nationalist leader Marcus Garvey died in London on 10 June 1940, Dr Moody wrote a moving tribute in the League's *News Letter*. He described Garvey as one of the greatest men the League had been associated with: 'No other man operating outside Africa has so far been able to unite our people in such large numbers for any object whatsoever.'[14]

At the height of the London Blitz, in addition to his work as a GP and a campaigner, Dr Moody continued to produce the League's monthly *News Letter*, and in an editorial he said: 'our work, such as the preparation of this letter, has to be carried on to the hum of hostile planes and the boom of friendly guns.'[15]

Dr Moody's influence continued to grow. He accepted an invitation to visit Buckingham Palace on 12 December 1940. On this occasion Her Majesty the Queen (the present queen's mother) received a fleet of thirty-five mobile canteens in the forecourt of Buckingham Palace. The mobile canteens had been purchased and provided by the colonies on behalf of Britain. Dr Moody's life-long friend and biographer, David A. Vaughan, described this important occasion in *Negro Victory* (1950), his biography of Dr Moody: 'During the ceremony Moody was presented to the Queen [who] made enquiries concerning the welfare of the people of his race and displayed a real interest in them.'[16] The League's *News Letter* said: 'The canteens will serve hot drinks and food to people in London and other cities who have been bombed out of their homes, or who, during the winter, have to spend long and anxious nights in shelters away from their homes.'[17]

Dr Moody also continued his medical work. In 1944 he was one of the first on the scene of the terrible V2 rocket incident in New Cross. Nearly 200 were killed and hundreds injured, mainly mothers and their children among the Christmas-shopping crowds. Dr Moody attended as part of a team called in from the surrounding area. They struggled night and day amidst the chaos and carnage to bring comfort to the survivors.

Basil Rodgers (Conscientious Objector)

In 1941 the League offered the post of travelling secretary to Basil Rodgers who had been a member of the organisation from its inception. Rodgers had been born in 1900 in Devon to a Jamaican father, the cabinet maker John Rodgers, and an English mother, Susan, who had also been born in Devon. By 1941 Rodgers had become a well-known singer (tenor). In the 1930s he had given concerts and recitals at Wigmore Hall in London. In 1932 a favourable review in *The Times* newspaper described the 'beautiful quality' of Rodgers' singing.[18] In October 1941 the League's *News Letter* profiled Rodgers and acknowledged that:

> He recently appeared before a tribunal in Bristol to answer as a conscientious objector to war. The learned judge stated that he had no doubt whatsoever about the sincerity of his convictions and gave him exemption to do the important work of Travelling Secretary to the League or failing that to carry on with his own present occupation. Mr. Rodgers feels, to quote his own words: 'that it is not enough to win the soil of a country, you must win the love and loyalty of its people. In the peace that is bound to come this love can never be won unless we, the coloured peoples, are represented not as serfs, but as equal partners in a great Commonwealth to carry out the Christian duty of the uplift of man.'[19]

However, Rodgers declined the offer of travelling secretary. In the *News Letter* he explained his reasons:

> It is with deep regret, owing to the events of war and the fact that war brings out the worst characteristics possible from the otherwise human race that I find it impossible to become an active paid member of any organisation, without indirectly becoming part of the war machine, and unless one can feel that he is at one with his colleagues, in every detail, such a job as defending the rights of coloured people would be out of the question.[20]

Rodgers died in Plymouth in 1983.

After the Second World War

As the war drew to a close, Dr Moody made a broadcast for the BBC in their series *Calling the West Indies* (13 May 1945). 'VE Day has come and gone,' he told listeners:

> The years of blood and toil and sweat have come to an end in Europe. The tension of war for millions is over. We are free again in the Continent of Europe. I have been in the midst of a peoples whose homes have been shattered, whose families have been battered, who themselves have been maimed. I have seen these people bear all these shocks bravely and with stoic resistance. I now see these same people breathing the air of relief, and, in their rejoicing, lighting those fires the sight of which, a while ago, would have struck them with terror ... I have rejoiced in meeting from time to time the fine group of men and women you have sent over from the West Indies, British Guiana and British Honduras. Their doings and achievements have thrilled me beyond telling. They will be coming back to you, we hope, before very long now, just as I hope my five boys and girls in the Services will be back again soon. They have all done magnificently as they battled against evil things. Now they and you will have to continue the war against those evil things which are hindering the progress and development of our beloved lands in the West Indies.[21]

In the winter of 1946–47 Dr Moody made a strenuous five-month tour of the United States and Caribbean. He wanted to raise money for a colonial culture centre in London. The 'speaking and preaching' tour exhausted him and he was disappointed that so little money had been raised. In ill-health, Dr Moody returned home to Peckham and died of acute influenza at 164 Queen's Road on 24 April 1947 at the age of 64. Thousands of people from all walks of life, including many of his patients, paid their respects at his funeral service which was held at the Camberwell Green Congregational Church on 1 May.

In his biography of Moody, David A. Vaughan described him as the leader of his people in the mother country and revealed that, during the war, he never neglected the easily forgotten small communities of black people living in seaport towns. For example, a group of 200 Africans had been stranded in Newcastle at the start of the war where they were often lonely and unhappy because of their feeling of isolation from the social life of the local community. Following an appeal from them, in 1941 Dr Moody travelled to Newcastle and met with a group of eleven representatives, including Charles Minto (see Chapter 2), who had organised the International Coloured Mutual Aid Association. A report in the League's *News Letter* said: 'They felt very keenly their isolation ... They felt that if Britain was really fighting for freedom she should begin by delivering them from slavery under which they now existed. "We put up with it with a smile and work away because we are Christians, but we long for better conditions." They appealed to the League to do something for them.'[22] The group derived much benefit and encouragement from Moody's visit.

Vaughan added that Moody gave to the League of Coloured Peoples 'devotion, sacrifice, passion and zeal for the rest of his life and he held the office of President continuously until his death in 1947. In many senses the League was his life and it would not be untrue to say that he was the life of the League.'[23] The League continued campaigning for several years after Dr Moody died, but went into decline at the time of the post-war increase of African and Caribbean settlers in Britain; although it is likely they could have benefited from an organisation that represented their interests and campaigned on their behalf.

In 1995 an English Heritage Blue Plaque was erected on Dr Moody's Peckham home, 164 Queen's Road, and in 2009 Ronald Moody's 1946 bronze portrait of his brother was given a permanent home in Peckham Library.[24]

CHAPTER 2

LEADING AND INSPIRING THE COMMUNITY

Wartime Britain was not without racism and a number of people worked hard to bring an end to discrimination. Black citizens with positions of responsibility and access to the government, Ministry of Labour or local authorities became representatives for the black community, though few have been given recognition for their efforts.

Ivor Cummings

Ivor Cummings, born in West Hartlepool in 1913, was a black Briton whose wartime role as the assistant welfare officer for the Colonial Office earned him a reputation as someone who would assist any black person in trouble. Before the war, in 1935, he found employment as the resident secretary and housekeeper of Aggrey House, a centre for colonial students, mostly from Africa and the West Indies, set up by the government in Bloomsbury, central London. When the war broke out he joined the Colonial Office, and though he received an OBE in 1947 for his war work, Ivor is barely mentioned in any histories of black people in Britain, including Peter Fryer's *Staying Power* (1984). Unlike his wartime contemporaries, Learie Constantine (see below) and Dr Harold Moody (see Chapter 1), Ivor has no entry in *The Oxford Companion to Black British History* (2007).

After his death in 1992, Ivor's obituarist Val Wilmer described him as 'a civil servant in the Colonial Office with special responsibilities for Commonwealth citizens', but though he was employed in an official capacity, 'the diligence and sensitivity with which he pursued his lifetime's work in the service of people of African descent were rooted in his own diffi-cult background and personal experience'.[1] Wilmer also acknowledged that Cummings was gay, while another source describes him as 'a fastidious, ele-gant man, with a manner reminiscent of Noel Coward – he chain smoked with a long cigarette holder and addressed visitors as "dear boy"'.[2]

Ivor's mother was an English nurse and his father, Ishmael Cummings, a doctor from Sierra Leone. When Dr Cummings returned to Africa, Ivor and his mother moved to Surrey where they became friends with the widow of the black Edwardian composer Samuel Coleridge-Taylor, and their two children Avril and Hiawatha. Though Ivor was educated at the prestigious Dulwich College in south London, poverty prevented him from pursuing a career as a doctor. In conversation with the writer Mike Phillips in the 1970s, Cummings revealed that he had been denied a commission at the start of the war because of a rule in the King's Regulations which stated that HM's offic-ers had to be of pure European descent. This was abandoned shortly after, but by then Cummings had accepted a post in the Civil Service.[3]

In 1941, as a spokesperson of the Colonial Office, Cummings visited the East End of London to investigate complaints he had received from the representative of a group of African and West Indian merchant seamen and workers from the Beckton Gas Works. In his report of the visit, dated 19 May 1941, Cummings described how he had travelled to Aldgate two days earlier and about forty-five men had turned up to the meeting to discuss their prob-lems. Their chief complaints were, in order of importance, that they had no meeting place, which forced them onto the streets night after night, making them vulnerable to police harassment; that they faced a 'colour bar' in some air-raid shelters; and that the Air Raid Precautions (ARP) authorities had offered them a separate shelter to themselves, which was proclaimed to be inferior and vulnerable to bombs. He reported: 'They seemed very anxious that I should see the Chief Warden on the subject, and they urged that I should attend to it at once.' They also spoke at length about police harass-ment. The police were very hard on them and would arrest them for trivial offences or incidents. Cummings stressed the need for action and recom-mended a 'thorough discussion' with the British Sailor's Society about the position of African and West Indian seamen in the Port of London, and that some consideration should be given to the provision of a club for the men: 'I considered them a good type and I believe that they would make an excel-lent Club if they were given the opportunity. Something very modest would do.' Regarding the discrimination in the air-raid shelters, Cummings pro-posed to get further evidence before the ARP authorities were approached. He had had previous experience of police harassment when he worked for Aggrey House in the 1930s. 'Complaints reached me that coloured people in the Tottenham Court Road area were being unduly molested by the police,' he said. With regard to the situation in 1941, he proposed the same direct action he took in the 1930s: 'I went to the Police Station and brought the matter up before the Superintendent. This had a good effect … Therefore in this matter I think a similar course of action would have the desired effect.' Cummings concluded that the men were 'most anxious for me to visit them again soon … I am very anxious not to lose touch with them'.[4]

In 1948, when Cummings was at Tilbury to meet the passengers of the *Empire Windrush*:

> he addressed the migrants in a tone of patronising kindliness which exactly echoed the spirit of the time. 'I now want to address my friends who have nowhere to go and no plans whatsoever. I am afraid you will have many difficulties, but I feel sure that with the right spirit and by cooperating as I have suggested above, you will overcome them.' On the surface he maintained an iron neutrality as befitted a senior Civil Servant. But in conversation with Mike Phillips in the seventies he revealed that, at the time, he was desperately anxious about the migrants' prospects.[5]

Rudolph Dunbar

The Guyanese clarinettist and conductor Rudolph Dunbar settled in London in the early 1930s where he founded the Rudolph Dunbar School of Clarinet Playing.[6] He continued to teach throughout the 1930s but he was also active in the jazz world. In 1932 Dunbar became the London correspondent of the Associated Negro Press (ANP), a national and international news agency for black newspapers which was established in Chicago in 1919. Dunbar continued to hold this post throughout the Second World War, working for the ANP as a war correspondent with the American 8th Army. In 1944 he crossed the Channel on D-Day and took part in the Normandy landings with a black regiment.

Also during the war, Dunbar worked for the British Ministry of Information with Learie Constantine to support West Indian munitions factory workers. In 1941 the Colonial Office encouraged Dunbar to support a black British perspective in African American newspapers and promote his roles as a conductor and radio broadcaster for the BBC in the hope of boosting morale in the colonies. In 1942 Dunbar made his London conducting debut with the London Philharmonic Orchestra at the Royal Albert Hall. It was a historic occasion, attended by an audience of over 7,000. He continued to tour as a guest conductor, notably with the Berlin Philharmonic in 1945. Also in

1945, Dunbar became the first foreigner to conduct a symphony orchestra in liberated Paris. The programme included the premiere of William Grant Still's *In Memoriam – The Colored Soldiers Who Died for Democracy*. His nephew Professor Ian Hall later recalled: 'In Paris he triumphed. He performed with various ensembles and Madame Debussy no less took him under her wing so he was a celebrated person.'[7]

After the war, as offers declined, Dunbar grew increasingly introspective. Hall said that Dunbar saw himself as the great maestro conductor, but opportunities to conduct were sporadic. He also described Dunbar as an 'enigma':

> On the one hand he was the English gent, very courteous and polite. He kissed the hands of women. Then there was an enormous contradiction. He was very bitter, depressed and unhappy about the way he had been treated. Towards the end of his life he was a figure of great pathos. His interests tended to diminish in number. He became obsessed with the idea that one day he would get this call from the BBC to conduct the BBC Concert Orchestra which, of course, wasn't going to happen. But he never fully accepted this.[8]

Pastor Daniels Ekarte (Liverpool)

Pastor Daniels Ekarte, who came to Britain from Nigeria, was a minister and community leader. In 1931 he opened the African Churches Mission in Toxteth, Liverpool. This provided a space for worship and socialising for the area's black community. In the 1940s three future African prime ministers stayed at the mission: Hastings Banda, Jomo Kenyatta and Kwame Nkrumah. As an air-raid warden during the war, Ekarte provided shelter for families who had lost their homes in the bombing. He accomplished this with little financial assistance, but with support from the local community, white and black, and some donations from local shopkeepers. In 1940 Ekarte lent his support to a strike by African seamen who were demanding higher wages and the end of the system whereby deductions were made for the shipping company's Liverpool hostel, whether the seamen stayed there or not. The men's demands were ignored. Ekarte also became involved in the welfare of 'brown babies', the 650 or so mixed race children who had been fathered by African American servicemen stationed in wartime Britain. The American army would not permit the men to marry the white mothers, so Ekarte lobbied the government for action on the children's behalf. He even gave shelter to some of them at the mission. With the help and support from the fund-raising efforts of Learie Constantine, Ekarte tried to purchase a larger property to use as a children's home, but the government did nothing to help them and Ekarte was not able to raise the money required. In a dawn raid the eight children at the mission were dragged away and dispersed around the country by Liverpool social services. Ekarte died in 1964.[9]

Charles Minto (North Shields)

During the war the Colonial Office opened several hostels for African seamen at various ports in England. In 1942, with the support of the Colonial Office, Charles Minto, an ex-boxer from Calabar, Nigeria, opened a hostel in North Shields for 200 African seamen who had been stranded there at the outbreak of war.[10] Minto found that the African seamen were living in poor conditions, had no one to organise them and no leader to plead for their rights. They had little or no contact with each other and were misunderstood by the local white community. They were unable to find employment because, as seamen, it was thought that they were only capable of undertaking jobs on board ships. At first, Minto had great difficulty in organising the men, but with patience he managed to bring them together. He also persuaded white employers to give them a chance.[11] Colonial House, described in the *Shields Evening News* as 'a splendid hostel with ideal recreational facilities – for the use of coloured seamen and other coloured people', was officially opened at 3 Northumberland Place, North Shields, on 1 May 1942 by Harold Macmillan MP, the parliamentary undersecretary for the colonies and a future Conservative prime minister (1957–63). Minto, described as the president of the International Coloured Mutual Aid Association, was also in attendance. In 1949 Charles Minto was recognised in King George VI's New Year's Honours List with an MBE for his work on behalf of the black community in North Shields. He died in 1960.

William 'Bill' Miller (Plymouth)

William 'Bill' Miller, the grandson of a freed slave, was born in Plymouth and was a Labour councillor and alderman there from the 1920s.[12] As early as 1938 Bill criticised Plymouth City Council's ill-conceived preparations for German air raids on the city. 'There has been muddle, drift and incompetency,' he said.[13] He expressed his concerns that the council were unprepared for bombing raids and he advocated the evacuation of the civilian population: 'It will be essential, for instance, to evacuate the public … There may be an opportunity for getting our people out of all this slaughter.'[14] Bill's concerns were ignored by the council, and he immediately joined the Civil Defence Warden's Service.

Bill's fears were realised after the fall of France in June 1940. Plymouth was one of the most vulnerable cities on the English coast. As an air-raid warden, Bill organised the evacuation of some local mothers and their children without orders:

> He commandeered buses, lorries and other vehicles and used them to take women and children to safe areas outside the city. The government had not authorised this evacuation. Bill was arrested for taking the law into his own hands and put on trial ... During the trial, he was asked why he had decided to organise the evacuation. He replied that he had told the men in his area who had gone away to fight in the war that he would do his best to protect their wives and families and this was the reason for his actions.[15]

Bill was found guilty by the tribunal. His punishment was a severe warning but three days later official evacuation began. Bill felt this vindicated his actions.

Bill was the head air-raid warden in Stonehouse during the heaviest bombing raids, which commenced in March 1941. The city was heavily bombed by the Luftwaffe in a series of raids known as the Plymouth Blitz. Although the dockyards were the principal targets, much of the city centre and over 3,700 houses were completely destroyed and more than 1,000 civilians lost their lives. Bill's own house in East Street was hit by a bomb in 1941 and he suffered temporary hearing loss as a result. His sister-in-law was severely injured and his two younger children had slight injuries. Bill remained head warden in Stonehouse until August 1941, but at a crucial time during the Plymouth Blitz he displayed great dedication and played an important role in the organisation of the local warden service. He also persuaded the army to provide field kitchens in the streets to feed the people and obtained the help of the marines in clearing the debris left by the air raids.

The air raids left Plymouth devastated: its population was reduced by almost half and the city centre had been destroyed. After the war Bill became the leading figure in Plymouth's ambitious housing reconstruction. In the 1946 New Year's Honours List, Bill was awarded a British Empire Medal. He received an OBE in 1947 and was given a CBE in 1948. He became Deputy Lord Mayor of Plymouth in 1962 and died in 1970 at the age of 80. His son Claude described his father as a very kind and gentle man: 'He didn't do anyone any harm. He was respected. A man of the people. You couldn't go for a walk with him in Plymouth because people would stop him and want to talk to him. One of the reasons he isn't better known is that historians take more notice of people from London.'[16]

Ernest Marke (London's West End)

Ernest Marke first landed in Britain in 1917 at the age of 15 after he stowed away from Freetown, Sierra Leone, on a merchant ship bound for Liverpool.[17] He has been described as a 'self made man' who lived by his wits.[18] He was originally a seafarer who spent more than a decade travelling around the world before settling in London, where he owned several West End night-clubs during the war. He bought a club at 5 Gerard Street and in 1940 he opened another club at New Compton Street. He once recalled:

> My Gerrard Street customers were mainly American GIs who were very vio-lent. But business was booming. I used to hire West Indian musicians who made all the difference. As for violence and crooked business from those bloody GIs, it didn't scare a strand of hair on my head because I had been baptised with it on the first night I landed in Harlem, New York in 1920.[19]

Marke was also a socialist and always concerned himself with the welfare of black people in Britain. Towards the end of the war, in 1944, he organ-ised the Coloured Workers Association and fund-raised for the defence of Philip Berry, an African American GI accused of murdering a white man who had molested another black GI escorting a white woman. On Sundays, his Gerard Street club was reserved for political discussions. Among the regular visitors to these gatherings were two budding African nationalists: Kwame Nkrumah and Jomo Kenyatta. They subsequently became presidents of Ghana and Kenya respectively. These Sunday meetings laid the foundation for the Pan-African Conference in Manchester in 1945. Marke published two autobiographies and died in 1995 at the age of 93.

Learie Constantine

Learie Constantine was perhaps the most famous black man in wartime Britain.[20] Born in Trinidad, Constantine was the grandson of slaves taken from Nigeria and he later commented on the role of Britain in the Trans-Atlantic Slave Trade: 'They destroyed the African background entirely so that if as Africans we live in the West Indies we are therefore taught how to forget Africa and one of the great things in my life is that I have *not* forgotten Africa and I will never forget Africa.'[21]

In the 1930s Constantine, popularly known as 'Connie', was among the best-paid sportsmen in Britain. As a first-class cricketer he accepted an offer from Nelson, a prominent Lancashire league team, to play for them in a professional capacity. He settled in Nelson in 1929. He played for them for eight seasons until 1937, and made the town his home until 1949. He welcomed a number of black visitors to his home, including fellow Trinidadian and cricket enthusiast, the historian, novelist and philosopher, C.L.R. James. In 1933 James helped Constantine to write his first book *Cricket and I*. Constantine later reflected on his responsibility as the first black professional cricketer who came to the Lancashire league: 'I had a job to do to satisfy people. I was as human as they were … I had to set an example … I carried a burden but I was helped tremendously by my wife … I felt as a pioneer I had to leave something creditable behind.'[22]

When war broke out, Constantine could have taken his wife Norma and young daughter Gloria to the safety of Trinidad, but he believed he owed something to the country that had adopted him. He said: 'I couldn't run away. I had got a standard of life in England that I could never have achieved in my country. I had made a lot of friends. England to me stood for something and now that war had started I would have felt like a little dog to have run away from England.'[23] The Constantine family stayed.

In Nelson, Constantine helped to prepare the local community for war by sandbagging a local hospital and volunteering as an air-raid equipment officer, although it turned out that Nelson was never bombed. He also accepted a job as a billeting officer. His duties included finding accommodation for servicemen who were stationed in the Nelson area, and inspecting and grading local houses in preparation for evacuees from Bradford and Manchester. Though nearly 40, Constantine expected to undertake some form of military service but instead he was offered a job as a welfare officer for the Ministry of Labour and National Service, in conjunction with the Colonial Office in the north-west region of England. His biographer, Gerald Howat, explained: 'His organisational ability, personal prestige, experience of Lancashire and racial background made him the ideal person to deal with the absorption of West Indians into the Merseyside industrial and social scene.'[24] It was a fairly senior but temporary Civil Service post. His main wartime role was to look after the interests of African seamen in Liverpool, and munitions workers and trainees from the West Indies in the north-west. Many of them had been hastily recruited from rural areas of the Caribbean. The government needed someone to act on their behalf and Constantine accepted. He was helped by an assistant, Sam Morris, who was active in the League of Coloured Peoples. The work began in October 1941 and Constantine was initially based in Liverpool's famous Royal Liver Building. It was in Liverpool that he experienced wartime bombing, but he was not troubled by the German air raids: 'I was a good sleeper in those days. I'd hear the siren but not the all clear because I had slept all through the bombing!'[25]

In Liverpool a great number of West Indians were employed as welders, tin plate workers and dockers in the Gladstone Docks. Sometimes, if there were racial tensions, Constantine intervened and mediated. It could be tough and demanding work, but he rose to the challenge: 'I had to do almost everything for them. I had to see they were comfortable in the factory. I had to make arrangements to see that they sent their money home. I had to look into the hostels that housed them while they were here. I had to help them to find digs when they were working in Birkenhead and places like that.'[26]

Even though the West Indians had travelled to England to help with the war effort, they often faced suspicion, hostility and discrimination in housing, wages and working conditions. Another Constantine biographer, Peter Mason, says:

> Most were ill equipped for life in the grey industrial north of wartime England, and at times their demands frustrated Constantine, who, as a hardened settler, found the naivety and niggles of the young immigrants rather taxing ... He was though, on the whole, deeply sympathetic to the plight of those he was asked to be an advocate for. They suffered many of the indignities that he had already experienced, yet without the buffer of his unusual status and financial comfort ... Although prepared to be outspoken, his preference was for talk rather than outright confrontation, and he was particularly successful in dealing with a strike of African merchant seamen, of whom there were also many based in Liverpool during the war.[27]

Constantine worked tirelessly on behalf of the West Indian war workers at various levels: with government departments, the League of Coloured Peoples, the churches and the United States forces. He also negotiated with trade unions and employers who flatly refused to employ black workers. In 1954 Constantine explained in his book *Colour Bar* that during the war older unions, such as the boilermakers', opposed black workers entering the industry because it had been difficult to find places in the industry for returning soldiers whose jobs had been taken by temporary workers during the First World War. They did not want the same thing to happen again. However, Constantine acknowledged that the electrical unions were more co-operative and black members took places on their union committees. Then there were those firms that either flatly refused to employ black workers, 'or put endless delays in their way hoping to make them seek work elsewhere. I used to get the Ministry to press those firms for most urgent deliveries of orders, and then they found that they must take some coloured workers or get none of any kind. With urgent work to be done, they were forced to give way.'[28]

On other occasions Constantine had to negotiate with some white hostel residents when they objected to sharing their accommodation with black workers. Once, Constantine took a private room in one of the hostels so that 'the white workers could see that I was an ordinary person like themselves and then might be willing to try some other coloured people as acquaintances'.[29]

However, though the experiment proved successful, while staying at the hostel Constantine ran into trouble one evening when he joined some friends at the dance hall. An American Air Force officer shouted at him to get out of the hall: 'we don't allow nigs to mix with white people where we are'. When Constantine politely asked the man to go away, the American replied: 'Get out nigger, before I smash you.' Constantine came close to hitting the American but realised that the newspaper headlines would have inflamed the situation as well as the hostility directed at West Indian workers and service-men from some white American troops. Peter Mason says:

> He always preferred a mannered response rather than an off-the-cuff aggressive reaction, reasoning that it worked better to portray the aggressor as undignified and unreasoning – to show that it was the perpetrator who was the sad victim of racism, not himself … Sam Morris said that while most [West Indians] 'paid him the greatest respect as an understanding elder brother figure, some were sceptical … of his genuineness and dubbed him a black Englishman'.[30]

Constantine made regular wartime broadcasts for the BBC to the Caribbean and to listeners in Britain. However, in 1943, when he submitted a script on racism in Britain to G.R. Barnes, who was the BBC's director of talks, it was rejected. Barnes considered it 'too controversial' for the series *Sunday Postscript*:

> You will remember that the object of that series is to stress unity rather than diversity … The emphasis on 'The tragedy of my race' seems to me to need relief and I should have thought that this could be obtained by inserting a passage somewhere to show that a little of the joy of living peeps through sometimes. With a British audience I should have thought far more sympathy would be obtained if the speaker identified himself with his audience by describing, for instance, some of the joy of first-class cricket.

Barnes then added that he would accept the script for a weekday broadcast if Constantine's 'ministry' and the Colonial Office passed it.[31]

Before the war, Constantine had been seen as a cricketer in several newsreel films, and during the war he took part in a couple of important documentary film shorts, made for propaganda purposes: *West Indies Calling* (1943) and

Learie Constantine (1944) (see Chapter 10). He also gave lectures to the forces, made hospital visits and played in charity cricket matches. A cricket match at Colwyn Bay in 1943 raised nearly £4,000 for the Red Cross prisoner-of-war fund. Through his work as a community leader and broadcaster, Constantine was one of the most famous, respected and inspirational black men in Britain in the war years. However, his position did not protect him from an act of overt racism he experienced in London in 1943.

There was to be an international cricket match at Lord's on 2 August and Constantine was given special leave from his war duties to take part. On arriving in London with his wife and daughter on 30 July, Constantine and his family were refused entry to the Imperial Hotel in Russell Square. The hotel feared that American guests would object to having black guests among them. The historian David Killingray explains: 'On arrival at the hotel he was told in insulting terms by the woman manager that "we will not have niggers in the hotel because of the Americans" … The interests of racially prejudiced white customers were then commonly used as an excuse to exclude non-white people from hotels, restaurants, and dances.'[32] Constantine took the hotel to court and he won the much-publicised case *Constantine* v. *Imperial Hotel, London* (1944).[33] However, many other black people were not so fortunate when they complained of racism in the forces and factories. Giving judgement to the Constantine case, Mr Justice Birkett described the hotel manageress as a 'lamentable figure in the witness box … She was grossly insulting in her reference to Mr Constantine, and her evidence is unworthy of credence.' He added that Constantine 'bore himself with modesty and dignity, and dealt with questions with intelligence and truth'.[34] In spite of the problems he encountered, when he was interviewed for *Calypso for Constantine* in 1966 he spoke positively about the war years: 'All the people in England had a comradeship which you wouldn't be able to appreciate now. Everybody was one. Everybody was smiling in the face of adversity. I just wish we could recapture that spirit in England.'[35] When Roy Plomley interviewed him in the popular BBC radio series *Desert Island Discs*, on 4 February 1963, Constantine told the presenter his luxury on the desert island would be a cricket ball 'with a little tallow to put around it and keep the twine fresh for as long as possible, so that I could always be fingering it and taking me back to days that made me so happy'. Constantine died in London in 1971 and a state funeral took place in Trinidad. He was posthumously awarded the Trinidad cross and there was a memorial service in Westminster Abbey.[36]

CHAPTER 3

KEEP SMILING THROUGH:
BLACK WOMEN IN WARTIME BRITAIN

There has never been a book written about the history of black women in Britain, and yet they have been living and working here since at least the early sixteenth century. Only one black woman from British history has been recognised: Mary Seacole (1805–81), a Jamaican 'doctress' who travelled at her own expense to the battlefields of the Crimean War of the 1850s. Seacole's autobiography was published in 1857 but, in spite of its success, she remained a forgotten figure until the 1980s when new interest was shown in her following a reprint of her book.[1] Since that time, Seacole has been included in the British school curriculum and, to date, she is the only black British historical figure to be given recognition. Others include the African Americans Martin Luther King Jr and Rosa Parks, and the South African Nelson Mandela. Because of her inclusion in the school curriculum, a number of books have been published about Seacole, aimed at young readers. However, in 2004, when Jane Robinson wrote the first full-length biography of Seacole, *Mary Seacole – The Most Famous Black Woman of the Victorian Age*, she was not placed in the context of other black Victorians, such as the Shakespearean actor Ira Aldridge and the Fisk Jubilee Singers. Therefore, the book gives the impression that, as a black person, Seacole existed in isolation.[2]

The absence of black women from British history books and other sources has made it extremely difficult to find information about the roles they played in British society. The historian Delia Jarrett-Macauley made this observation in 1996 when she described the black woman as 'losing her place in British history. It is hardly ever remembered that she played an active part within the Second World War, in the services, in munitions factories, in the media and in a multitude of other areas of life.'[3] This is hardly surprising, given that British history books are largely researched and written by historians from white, male, middle-class backgrounds.

There were probably several thousand black and mixed race women living in Britain at the start of the war. Many more arrived from the West Indies during the war to join the services, including the ATS (Auxiliary Territorial Service). Black women also worked on the land, in munitions factories and as nurses. The individual experiences of these women were varied, and they existed in all social classes, but information is hard to find.

In 1991 Ben Bousquet and Colin Douglas' book, *West Indian Women at War – British Racism in World War II*, was a landmark publication which documented the role of black women from the West Indies who enlisted in the ATS. It also included the story of one British-born black servicewoman, Lilian Bader, but it was not Ben and Colin's intention to include black women on the home front. However, they did point out that 'in war, the woman's role is too quickly forgotten'.[4]

A Letter to Winston Churchill

In 1941 Britain's prime minister, Winston Churchill, received a letter from a black housewife who was living in poor accommodation in Camden Town, London. Mrs Uroom described herself as the daughter of an Englishwoman and a West Indian father, and married to a West African who was employed on demolition work. In her letter, dated 10 October 1941, Mrs Uroom pleaded with the prime minister to address the discrimination faced by some black British citizens in wartime. She asked why black people had to suffer because there were no 'decent' places for them to live. She explained that every agent black people approached for a room refused them while other 'nationalities' could get places to live. 'Can't something be done about coloured peoples,' she asked. 'After all, we are British subjects. If this letter is received by you I hope it will not be cast aside.'[5]

The letter was not cast aside but forwarded by the prime minister to the Social Services Department of Downing Street. In a reply to Mrs Uroom, dated October 1941, it is suggested that she make an appointment with John L. Keith, a welfare officer in the Colonial Office, to discuss with him the issues she raised. The Oxford-educated Keith had joined the Colonial Office in 1939 and in 1941 he became the director of colonial scholars and head of the student department, a post he held for fifteen years. During the war years, Keith investigated the problems faced by many members of Britain's black community, maintaining a liberal approach to the situations he encountered.

Following the meeting with Mrs Uroom, Keith drafted a report on 29 October 1941 in which he described her as 'an intelligent and sensible woman ... She told me about the difficulties which working-class coloured people have in finding decent and reasonably priced accommodation in London.' Mrs Uroom also alleged that black people in the Camden Town area were badly treated by air-raid wardens and police officers who ejected them from air-raid shelters and the tube 'as if they were Jews in Germany'.[6] Keith advised Mrs Uroom to encourage black people who had been subjected to acts of racism to come and see him at the Colonial Office and he assured her that he would discuss her complaints with the chief warden of the Camden Town ARP and a senior police officer.

Amelia King and the Women's Land Army

In June 1939 the Ministry of Agriculture decided to recreate the Women's Land Army – a throw-back to the First World War. By August that year the Women's Land Army had 30,000 recruits. However, when Amelia King, a young black woman from Stepney in the East End of London, volunteered to join she was turned down. While her father was serving in the Merchant Navy and her brother in the Royal Navy, Amelia was rejected by its Essex County Committee because she was black. It was alleged that some farmers had raised objections to her. Some of the locals on whom she might have been billeted had also objected. Amelia's predicament was raised by Walter Edwards in the House of Commons. The Conservative Minister of Agriculture, Robert Hudson, made excuses: 'Careful enquiry has been made into the possibility of finding employment and a billet for Miss King, but when it became apparent that this was likely to prove extremely difficult, she was advised to volunteer for other war work where her services could be more speedily utilised.' Mr Edwards responded: 'In view of the insult that has been passed to this girl and to her father and brother, both of whom are doing valuable war work, cannot the Minister do something about the farmers who are responsible for this position?' Mr Hudson replied: 'I do not employ members of the Women's Land Army. It is not like other Women's Services.' When questioned he said that he did not endorse the colour bar. Another MP, Mr Lawson, told Hudson that 'the world listens to matters of this kind, which affect the integrity of the British people', but Hudson made no reply.[7]

The racism experienced by Amelia King aroused feelings of anger in many British people. In one poll carried out by the public opinion organisation Mass Observation, 49 per cent of the 62 per cent who had heard about Amelia 'strongly disapproved', while a further 12 per cent 'disapproved'. A rider was added that 'even those who did not entirely believe in colour equality were against this particular case of colour prejudice which was regarded as detrimental to the war effort'.[8]

A Long, Long Trip: West Indian and African American Servicewomen in Britain

The majority of white Britons had not come into contact with black women before the war and, if the War Office had had its way, the situation would have stayed the same. However, in 1943, as the war intensified, this particular 'colour bar' ended and West Indian women were invited to join the ATS. The black West Indian ATS was sent to Britain, while the white West Indian ATS was posted to Washington DC. The Americans refused to accept black West Indians.[9]

The response was immediate and some West Indian women were so keen to 'join up' that they were prepared to pay for their passage to Britain. The women who were recruited to the ATS began to arrive in Britain in October 1943. Ben Bousquet commented: 'Women actually paid their way across to fight for King and country. They were nice middle-class black women who wouldn't have done anything anyway other than stay at home. So the war was a form of elevation, a release.'[10] Among the recruits was Norma Best from Trinidad: 'I thought this is an opportunity for me to see the world and also do my service for dear old England. That was very important to me and for my family. We were very loyal people. Also my father had served in the trenches in the First World War.'[11] Nadia Cattouse, from British Honduras (now Belize), a British colony in Central America, also volunteered for the ATS: 'In 1943 they asked for volunteers. I heard it on the local news and I was so eager I jumped on my bike straight away to get to Drill Hall.'[12] Nadia was signed up and soon joined a group of other West Indian volunteers to travel to Britain, but they had to go via Miami, Florida. The young women were unprepared for the racism they encountered on the journey.

In Miami the hotel booked for them by the British army refused to take them in. The following day an ATS officer arrived from Washington and took the women to another hotel where the manager was a Scotsman. He agreed to take them in as long as they did not enter his hotel by the front door. At the railway station there were two queues for the Washington train: one for whites; the other for blacks. Unused to racial segregation in the West Indies, the women defiantly joined the white queue. The African Americans they encountered in the 'Jim Crow' (racially segregated) queue expressed their concerns that something bad could happen to the women. On the train, which was also racially segregated, a compromise was reached. Nadia and her fellow travellers were given a drawing-room to themselves: 'We refused to go to the Jim Crow car, and the black passengers who befriended us feared for our safety. Our defiant action predated Rosa Parks' refusal to give up her seat on a Jim Crow bus by at least ten years.'[13] In spite of their brave stand, when the women tried to enter the dining car they were turned away and had to buy their food from platform buffets.

Nadia arrived in England in June 1944:

> There were only six of us when I journeyed to England, and we arrived on a ship packed with thousands of American soldiers. I had no contact with American southerners. I was lucky! When our train arrived in London an air-raid siren went, and I was surprised that everyone strolled around so calm. I couldn't understand this. Then we were directed to an underground shelter. So my first impression of London is the air-raid siren! Eventually I went to Edinburgh for special training as a signals operator. In Edinburgh there was no racial tension. No problem at all. We had camaraderie.[14]

Though Ben Bousquet and Colin Douglas have made an extensive study of West Indian women in wartime, little acknowledgement has been given to the African American women who arrived in Birmingham in January and February 1945. It was the first time the American army had permitted black members of the Women's Army Corps (WAC) to serve overseas. An all-black unit called the 6888th Central Postal Directory Battalion was created, based first in Birmingham and then later in France. Their job was to route mail to millions of service personnel based in Europe. Much of it had been piling up in English warehouses.

The commander of the unit was Major Charity Adams, the first African American to be commissioned an officer in the WAC (in August 1942) and one of only two black women to hold a wartime rank in the WAC as high as major. In her autobiography, *One Woman's Army*, Major Adams recalled that when she arrived in London with members of the unit, having flown over in advance to make preparations for their stay in Birmingham: 'Suddenly, our minority status disappeared.' In London, Major Adams was impressed by the diversity of its people, 'and every conceivable kind of uniform could be seen on the streets, worn by all races, colors, shapes, sizes, sexes, and religious persuasions'.[15] Soon afterwards, Major Adams realised the dangers of being in a war zone. The unit had arrived in London during the period of the V-2 rockets, and witnessed the death and destruction they were causing:

I think my greatest personal admiration for the English, especially the Londoners, was at this time because they 'carried on' in spite of the V-2 bombs. Each morning when we went out, the streets had been cleared of the damage of the bombs of the night before, and the destruction had been boarded up out of sight from the street.[16]

When the over 700-strong 6888th postal unit arrived in Birmingham, they were the first black women many white people in the city had ever seen and they shattered the stereotypes. They had been greeted by Brigadier-General Benjamin O. Davis, the only black general in the American army, and it was reported on the front page of *The Birmingham Post* that they sung their own words to the marching song *There's a long, long trip we're taking*.[17] They were given a rousing welcome when they arrived in Birmingham. Crowds of locals came out to watch as the parade of black women passed by. *The Birmingham Sunday Mercury* commented: 'These WACS are very different from the coloured women portrayed on the films, where they are usually domestics or the outspoken old-retainer type … The WACS have dignity and proper reserve.'[18]

Chrissy Sinclair: From Show Girl to GI War Bride

At the outbreak of war, one of Britain's oldest black communities existed in Cardiff, South Wales. Butetown, situated close to the Cardiff docks, was home to a mixture of nationalities. Some of these were African and West Indian seamen who married white women and raised families. Until the regeneration of the area in the 1960s, the popular image of Butetown, or 'Tiger Bay', was an immoral hotbed of prostitution, gambling and violence. This racist view was perpetuated by tabloid newspapers and the media in general, but it was always strongly criticised and rejected by the people who lived there. What the media ignored was the strong feeling of solidarity that existed in Britain's most culturally diverse community. In Colin Prescod's documentary *Tiger Bay is My Home* (1984), the St Lucian seaman Kenneth Trotman said: 'You never miss your island when you're down in Butetown. Everybody lived like one big family. Don't matter what colour you was or where you were from. Everybody was one. I never was hungry once in Cardiff.'[19]

Chrissy Sinclair was born in Butetown in 1917 to Macdonald Sinclair, who came from Barbados, and his Welsh wife Margaret. Chrissy was just 2 years old when Butetown experienced the anti-black race riots. When Chrissy left school in the 1930s employment prospects for black and mixed race girls were extremely limited. However, there were always opportunities to be found in the world of entertainment. Chrissy was drawn to London's West End, in and around the streets of Soho near Piccadilly Circus. She became a showgirl and part of London's 'exotic' night life. Her father, born in the Victorian era, was enraged. For him, being a showgirl was no better than being a prostitute. Towards the end of the war, from June 1944 to January 1945, Chrissy was one of dozens of black extras and bit players who were employed at Denham Studios in Buckinghamshire on the film *Caesar and Cleopatra* (1945). She also met her husband, Henry Kennard, an African American army corporal based at Wattisham in Suffolk. He swept her off her feet, married her in London on 22 September 1945 and took her to his home in Boston, Massachusetts. Chrissy's nephew Neil takes up the story:

> Chrissy was among the first war brides to make the transatlantic crossing. On board the passenger vessel at Southampton was a military band, a ship load of people and the excitement of brides off to new lives. Of course they sang. 'Play Jerusalem!' she shouted. And they obliged. 'No, no,' she exclaimed, 'Not that one!' Then she sang, 'And did those feet in ancient times …' – and all the British brides joined in. With Chrissy singing 'Mae hen 'wlad fy nhadau' the ship departed.[20]

Chrissy didn't visit Tiger Bay again until 1958. She died in Boston in 1986 at the age of 69.[21]

Grace Wilkie: 'I Belong to Liverpool'

Grace Wilkie was born Grace Kie Walker in Liverpool in 1918 to an African seaman, Cratue Walker, and an English mother, Elizabeth Cropper. Soon after she was born, Grace's father left his wife and baby daughter to go to America. He never returned. In the 1700s Liverpool had grown from an insignificant port to a wealthy city and the money came mainly from slavery. Elizabeth was descended from the Cropper family of Dingle Bank, an old Liverpool family. In the 1700s they went to Jamaica and purchased slaves, not for themselves, but to bring them to England, to release them and find work for them. James Cropper, one of Grace's ancestors, joined the movement to abolish slavery, but the Cropper family did not carry on with their liberal tradition and raised objections to Elizabeth's marriage. Grace and her mother were rejected by members of the Cropper family. Grace was 10 years old when her mother died and it was left to an uncle from Africa to teach the young girl various domestic chores, such as cooking and cleaning the house.

In 1991, when Grace was interviewed in the first edition of the BBC television series *Black Britain*, she recalled: 'At school we were taught to believe that Africans lived in little wooden huts. My uncle told me it wasn't so. He said a lot of people lived in the bush, but they did have cities for people to live in.' She also described the poverty that existed amongst Liverpool's working classes in the 1930s. Fathers pawned their suits, mothers starved to let their children eat. Grace remembered giving birth during an air raid on Liverpool on 10 January 1941:

> I became pregnant in 1940 and there was bombs dropping all over the place, anti aircraft guns going. It was terrible. And we had to have torchlight to bring my son Derry into the world because that night they dropped a bomb right behind where we lived. The hole in the ground was immense. It took away half the street. A lot of houses went that night. Some people got gassed on their premises and through all this I was giving birth to Derry. There was nothing I could do. There was no where I could go. It was a bad bad raid.

In the 1960s Derry Wilkie became well known on the Liverpool scene as a musician and was affectionately known as 'the black Beatle'. Grace died in 2002 at the age of 84. A Liverpudlian through and through, she said: 'I belong to Liverpool and Liverpool belongs to me.'[22]

Lilian Bader: Life in the Forces

Lilian Bader was born in Liverpool in 1918 to Marcus Bailey, from Barbados, who was serving in the Merchant Navy, and Lilian, a British-born woman of Irish parents.[23] Orphaned in January 1927 at the age of 8, Lilian was raised in a convent where she remained until she was 20 because no one would employ her. She made numerous attempts to secure a job and often experienced racism at interviews: 'you sit there looking very stoic, pretending you don't care, wishing you were out of it. Nobody would employ me, and that was when I realised I had a problem with colour.'[24] Eventually Lilian was employed in domestic service, but when the war broke out she was determined to leave domestic service and join the forces.

At first she joined the NAAFI at Catterick Camp, Yorkshire, and was enjoying herself until she was asked to leave when her father's background was discovered by an official in London. For weeks her supervisor avoided informing her of this decision, but eventually he had to tell her the truth and release her. Lilian later explained that this came about because of the hysteria in Britain in the early months of the war, 'when anyone who looked a bit foreign or different was treated with suspicion'.[25] She returned to domestic service and felt embarrassed when a group of soldiers at a gun post expressed surprise that she was not doing war work: 'How could I tell them that a coloured Briton was not acceptable, even in the humble NAAFI?'[26] Lilian was determined to join up after hearing the story of Dicken, who had been made deaf from the bombing at Dunkirk: 'He said, "Every time they kept telling us to bloody well dig in I found another dead body." So that really got me. I felt guilty I wasn't doing anything. So more than ever I wanted to do something.'[27] One day Lilian heard a group of West Indians being interviewed on the radio. When they wanted to volunteer and 'do their bit', they had been rejected by the army, but the Royal Air Force accepted them. Lilian enlisted with the Women's Auxiliary Air Force (WAAF) on 28 March 1941 and found herself 'the only coloured person in this sea of white faces', but 'somebody told me I looked smart in my uniform which cheered me no end'.[28]

Lilian's joy at being enlisted in the WAAF was overshadowed by tragedy. Just two weeks prior to enlisting, her older brother, Able Seaman James Bailey, was killed in action while serving in the Merchant Navy: 'My brother Jim had been reported missing, but I hoped against hope that he had been picked up as I knew he sailed in convoy. The survivors of his ship, the Western Chief, were picked up, but Jim was not amongst them.'[29] In December 1941 Lilian became a leading aircraftwoman (LACW) and soon gained the rank of acting corporal.

Through an ex-landlady in Yorkshire, Lilian made contact with a young British-born black soldier called Ramsay Bader of the Essex Yeomanry; letters and photographs were exchanged. Until then, Lilian had rarely encountered other black people, especially in the forces: 'It was a relief to meet a coloured boy-friend for a change. I had met no other coloured WAAFs, and only seen an Indian RAF officer and one coloured airman who appeared fleetingly at Condover.'[30] Lilian and Ramsay became engaged and were married in 1943 in Hull: 'We had a quiet little wedding: no music and no flowers on the altar … My wedding cake had a plaster of Paris top which when removed showed a chocolate or ginger cake! We spent the night at a hotel and Hitler duly celebrated with an air-raid.'[31]

Lilian's chances of further promotion in the WAAF were curtailed when she discovered she was expecting a baby. She received her discharge in February 1944. That same year Ramsay was one of thousands of soldiers engaged in the D-Day landings. It was an anxious time for Lilian:

For long periods you wouldn't get any news at all from the second front, the Normandy landings, because the mail didn't get through. At one stage I didn't know if Ramsay was alive or dead but you just kept going and I remember kneeling in the chapel and praying like blazers that Ramsay would be saved. It was a terrible time because you knew some people were going to be killed, and Ramsay couldn't swim! That's what worried me more than anything, but he came through.[32]

At the end of the war Lilian was living in Derby where black and white troops were stationed – and segregated. She recalled an ugly incident that occurred on VE night when she was subjected to abuse by a black American soldier who thought her baby was white. He probably had good cause to feel bitter and angry after suffering years of abuse from white GIs, but his outburst should not have been directed at Lilian, who was deeply upset and never had an opportunity to tell him she was proud to be both black and British, and to have served her country: 'On VE night we all dashed out into the streets and I was out with my pram … I'll never forget to this day a black face just pushing its way through the crowd and a voice said "yellow bitch" and that face vanished … that really shook me as I'd always been proud of my race.'[33] Lilian had two sons and trained to become a teacher. In 2008, at the age of 90, she travelled to London for the opening of the Imperial War Museum's 'War to Windrush' exhibition.

Barbara Carter: the 'Black Ambassadress'

Barbara Carter was born in British Guiana in 1914 and was in Europe with her musician husband, the Guyanese saxophonist Stanley Carter, and their baby daughter when war broke out. The Carters arrived in England in September 1939 and tried to find a hotel, without success. One commissioner at the doors of a hotel in Russell Square put it bluntly: 'We don't have niggers here.' While Stanley spent the war years entertaining the troops at camps around Britain, Barbara volunteered to work as a nursery nurse. Stanley's war service brought him into contact with black service personnel and some of them were invited to the Carter's home in London's Baker Street. Barbara, known as 'Babsy' to her friends, cooked and offered hospitality. One RAF serviceman from the West Indies said:

> Our main source of socialising was visiting each other. Babs' home was one of the principal meeting places. Many would give her name to the Red Cross when they had to go into active service. They had a nickname for her, the 'Black Ambassadress'. She received many telegrams telling of her friends' deaths and injuries in action.[34]

In contrast to the hostility faced during air raids by Mrs Uroom in Camden Town, Barbara and her young children were helped by their white neighbours when the Luftwaffe bombed London. Barbara's presence in her local air-raid shelter was also seen as good luck. When the air raids intensified, Barbara evacuated herself and her children to Wales. After the birth of her third child she returned to London where she kept her 'open door' policy to those black individuals who wanted a friendly place to visit, eat and meet other black service personnel, entertainers and academics. After the war she continued to offer support, advice and companionship to black settlers. Barbara, in her nineties at the time of writing, still lives in West London.

Pauline Henriques: 'An Interesting Novelty'

Pauline Henriques was born in Jamaica in 1914 and settled in St John's Wood, London, with her family when she was 5 years old.[35] Pauline's father, Cyril, was a successful import and export merchant and wanted his six children to have an English education. Pauline described him as 'a most interesting man. He was well educated, cultured and had a passion for reading, music and the theatre'.[36] One of Pauline's brothers, also Cyril, became Lord Chief Justice of Jamaica; he was knighted in 1963. Another, Fernando, was made president of the Oxford Union in 1944 and became professor of social anthropology at Sussex University.

At the outbreak of war Pauline was a 'comfortably off' young housewife, married to Geoffrey Henebery, an insurance clerk, with a 2-year-old daughter. The Heneberys had just moved into a flat in Hampstead when they heard Neville Chamberlain's famous speech in which he declared war on Germany: 'And then the air-raid warning sounded immediately after Chamberlain's speech, and we thought let's get out.'[37] The Heneberys climbed up Parliament Hill and watched barrage balloons rising across London: 'It was almost magical, although the implications were frightening … It was not really an air-raid warning. I think it was probably done to alert people to the importance of what had happened … In a funny sort of way, we really didn't have any knowledge of what was going to happen, so I don't think we were frightened.'[38] Pauline's parents had just returned to Jamaica and when the threat of war became a reality they asked her to stay with them: 'but I felt that my roots were here'.[39] Pauline didn't expect to join up: 'In those days when you married and had children you stayed at home. I took it for granted this was my role. In any case, at the beginning of the war, I was a pacifist and didn't entertain any thoughts of joining up.'[40]

Towards the end of 1939, when Geoffrey Henebery's employers relocated him to Carlisle, Cumbria, he took his family with him. Pauline described this as a totally new life, an 'absolute revelation'. In their first year there, Geoffrey was called up and joined the navy. Pauline found herself with time on her hands. She took in three evacuees, but mothers with young children were discouraged by the government from working, though many in this situation demanded to make a contribution to the war effort. In 1942 some young mothers marched with placards strapped to their prams and pushchairs demanding 'We want war work. We want nurseries'. Pauline was one of those young mothers who wanted to undertake war work even though she was taking care of a young daughter and evacuees: 'I didn't want just to be the housewife and keep cleaning the whole time. It seemed an unnecessary waste.'[41] She described the young mothers she befriended in Carlisle in the early years of the war as a 'little community' who were longing to do something for the war effort: 'One or two of them went to the Air Ministry and I thought I could do that, so I taught myself to type.'[42] Pauline found employment typing invoices for the Air Ministry. It was the first money she had ever earned, and she was thrilled with the independence it gave her. 'Then I found it was just lovely having my own money. I wasn't earning much, but just to be able to control it … I could never think of not earning money again.'[43]

Pauline was the only black person in Carlisle and proved to be very popular in her community. She said there were two reasons for this: being the only black person in the city (apart from some African American GIs who were billeted there after the United States entered the war in December 1941) and having a 'good speaking voice'. During the war Pauline realised her ambition to enter the theatre by working in her spare time as an actress and producer with the Carlisle Little Theatre, an amateur theatre company. She said she didn't encounter any racism at all: 'Everybody found it an interesting novelty to have a black woman involved. In Carlisle people were surprised to find this intelligent black woman working with a theatre company, keeping busy and active.'[44]

Pauline left Carlisle in 1944 and moved back to London. After the war, Pauline worked as an actress and broadcaster with BBC radio's West Indian and West African services. Her many appearances included the popular literary programme *Caribbean Voices*. When acting work proved difficult to find, Pauline turned her attention to social work. In 1966 she became Britain's first black woman magistrate and in 1969 she was awarded an OBE.

Towards the end of her life, Pauline reflected:

There was great relief when the war in Europe was over, but it was short-lived for me because of the shock of Hiroshima. I remember the news of that, and was just shattered by the horror, and what it was going to mean. It was just so, so awful ... Deep down I don't think I ever believed that the war was ever right, and I had kept this in my mind all along. I had always, throughout the war, stuck up for the pacifists.[45]

She died in 1998.

CHAPTER 4

ESTHER BRUCE:

A BLACK LONDONER AT WAR

Esther Bruce was a working-class Londoner whose life spanned almost the entire twentieth century: 1912–94.[1] At the outbreak of war, and with the threat of air raids and a Nazi invasion, Esther's Guyanese father Joseph tried to persuade her to leave Britain and travel to the country of his birth to live with his mother, but Esther was a young woman of 26 and had rarely left London. She refused to leave her father and the community in which she had been raised. Though she had been corresponding with her grandmother in British Guiana, she had never met her. Esther looked upon her neighbours in the Fulham community in which she lived as her extended family.

Esther Bruce's father Joseph had settled in Dieppe Street in the Fulham area of London during the Edwardian era when very few black people lived in Britain. He had travelled to London from British Guiana when it was part of the empire, a British colony in South America. He was a proud, independent man and it couldn't have been easy for him to leave his country and family behind, and settle in a white, working-class community. When he married Edith Brooks, and their daughter Esther was born, Joseph was working as a builder's labourer, but Esther's mother died when she was 5 and Joseph had to raise her alone.[2] Esther described her father as a proud man who was tough and could take care of himself. He always made a stand against acts of racism, especially when they were directed at his family. Esther left school at the age of 14 to work in service but she was exploited and mistreated by her employers. Her Guyanese step-mother, Jennie, taught her how to sew and she worked as a seamstress until she retired at the age of 74. Esther experienced overt racism in 1931 when she was sacked from a job for being 'coloured', but most of the time she integrated and made friends. In later years she spoke with fondness about the community spirit that existed in Fulham before and during the Second World War: 'In the old days the people of Fulham used to be one big happy family and we helped each other. We were poor but people cared about each other. People were friendly and that meant a lot.'[3]

In the 1930s Esther was employed as a seamstress and made dresses for the popular American singer Elisabeth Welch (see Chapter 8), and later in the decade she met and befriended the Jamaican Marcus Garvey in North End Road, Fulham. He is now recognised as the father of Black Nationalism and the most influential black activist of the twentieth century. The office of his organisation, Universal Negro Improvement Association (UNIA), at 2 Beaumont Crescent, backed onto Dieppe Street, and he lived nearby at 53 Talgarth Road until his death on 10 June 1940.[4] Esther said: 'Marcus Garvey was a nice chap who wasn't treated with respect like I was. He was middle-class and the costers in the market wouldn't speak to him. He told me the English are no good but I said there are *some* good people in this world.'[5]

Into the Blitz

When the war started Joseph and Esther were given gas marks, but she hated wearing it: 'It smelled of rubber. I only wore mine once.' The blackout made her laugh: 'In the war we had the blackout and you couldn't see each other in the street so if you walked into someone you'd say: "Sorry mate". Sometimes it was only a lamp post but you still said sorry! And then you'd laugh at yourself and say: "What's the matter with me? It was only a lamp post!"'[6]

When the air raids started Joseph stayed in the house. Esther said he took a chance, 'a lot of people did', but she played safe and went to the public shelter with her neighbours:

One night we all had to get out of there because the Germans surrounded it with incendiary bombs. They were fire bombs which the Germans were dropping so that the others who followed could find Earls Court, which was very close to where we lived. Later on a bomb landed right behind the shelter and didn't explode. Some people said they could hear it ticking. The air raid warden came in and told us we had to get out. I had an old girl sitting near me. That was poor old Mrs Clark. She said: 'Will you take me to the shelter at the other end of the street, Esther?' I said: 'Of course I will, love.' But it was quite a long way to the other shelter and the Germans were going hell for leather. Bombs were falling everywhere. Mrs Clark was hanging onto me. So we got out of the shelter in Eli Street and went with the neighbours through the air raid and into the one in Hilmer Street. It was packed. As for being scared, I just didn't think about it.[7]

Esther recalled the friendliness and community spirit that existed during the Blitz: 'You'd be walking along and the air raid siren would go, and people opened their doors and shouted: "Come in here, love" and they would give you shelter. People are not like that today. During the war people were very friendly. I think the war, in a way, made people more friendly but after the war people changed.'[8]

In the early part of the war women were encouraged to volunteer for war work, but in 1941 it became clear that more women were needed and they would have to be mobilised. In January 1941 there were 350,000 unemployed women in Britain, but most of these had found work by 1942. The government announced that all able-bodied people of both sexes would be required to undertake 'national service' and in 1941, with some reluctance, the government introduced conscription for unmarried women between the ages of 20 and 30. In 1941 Esther was required to leave her job as a seamstress to register for war work. She was offered a job in a munitions factory in Newcastle, but Esther said: 'I'm not leaving home.' They then offered her a job in the Land Army. She said: 'No, I don't want to get up at half past five to milk cows. That's not for me.' When she was asked what war work she *was* prepared to take, she replied: 'I'll have a bash in a hospital.'[9] So Esther went to work as a ward cleaner in Fulham Hospital.

In addition to cleaning hospital wards, Esther volunteered to work as a fire guard or fire watcher. This position came about as a result of the night of Sunday 29 December 1940, when the City of London was devastated by incendiary bombs, 18 inches long and weighing only a couple of pounds, but filled with highly combustible chemicals and dropped in clusters to spread fires. Soon after it had begun to burn – and while it was still possible for an individual to put it out with sand or a stirrup pump – it could explode, showering anyone trying to put it out with magnesium. When the fire watchers' scheme began in January 1941 it was made compulsory to have a person or persons on guard in buildings twenty-four hours a day (in 'prescribed areas') to put out incendiary bombs and to call for help. This proved difficult for many establishments to staff and led the government to implement a compulsory scheme of fire watching.

Armed with a stirrup pump, a helmet and an armband labelled 'Fire Guard', Esther's work involved standing on the roofs of Fulham and Brompton hospitals during air raids and helping to put out any fires caused by incendiaries. It was a hazardous job, and many women who had not enlisted in the armed forces volunteered. She said: 'It was dangerous work, and I didn't really want to do it, but when the air raids continued, we knew we would all have to do our bit, and pitch in.'[10]

After leaving Fulham Hospital, Esther spent the rest of the war in Brompton Hospital:

I cleaned three wards. One was called the forces ward. This is where they put boys who had been wounded serving with the army, navy and air force. I had a smashing time in there. The pranks those boys got up to! I had to clean the ward the old-fashioned way. Down on my hands and knees with the polish and the bumper. I had a lot of fun in the forces ward. When the boys knew I was coming back on duty for the evening shift they asked me to bring them fish and chips.[11]

In March 1941 tragedy struck when Joseph Bruce was involved in an accident in the blackout. He was knocked down and injured by a taxi during an air raid and taken by ambulance to a hospital in Windsor. He died from his injuries several days later at the age of 60. Esther recalled:

After Dad was killed, I was left on my own. I'd never lived on my own before and I hated it. So Granny Johnson asked me to come and live with her at 13 Dieppe Street. We'd been neighbours for years. She said: 'Come over here and live with me, Esther.' The war had started and food was rationed. It made sense. So I moved into 13 Dieppe Street and shared a room at the top of the house with Granny. She was like a mother to me. She was an angel.

Hannah Johnson was affectionately known in their community as 'Granny'. She was a mother figure to everyone, and greatly loved and respected. For Esther, Granny was a life saver and they took care of each other until Granny died on 7 November 1952 at the age of 75. Granny's granddaughter Kathy, born in 1931, lived with them at 13 Dieppe Street and remembers: 'They had a sense of fun and knew how to enjoy themselves. Gran and Esther got on well together, and they were together for a long time. Gran was like a mother to Esther ... As far as I can remember Esther was the only black person living in our area. She was part of our community. People knew her. She made friends with everyone. She was always chatting to someone in the street.'[12]

Granny's grandson Jack remembers the times he accompanied her and Esther to the 'pictures' during the war:

If I knew they were going I'd ask them to take me. Gawd did I love films. I went about four times a week if my mum gave me the money. We'd usually go to the Red Hall but, if they were full and queuing outside, me and Esther would try and rush Gran across the busy North End Road to where the Regal was located – no mean feat considering Gran's size. We hoped we'd get in to see a film there. The Regal was a lovely art deco style building. Now this you won't believe but it is true. Every time we went to the pictures Gran used to like to sit in the front row so she could stretch out her legs and she wouldn't need to get up from her seat to let anyone pass by. If Esther had taken Gran to see a war film Gran would shout out in the cinema for 'our boys' to 'kill the sods' (the Germans). She'd holler 'shoot the bleeders!' Esther would laugh out loud and so would our nearby audience, but for a young lad like me I found it all too embarrassing. [13]

Throughout the war, during air raids, it was important that everyone got on with each other, and Esther fondly recalled how Granny took care of her and how the air raids brought their community together, especially in their local air-raid shelter:

When I came home from work and went to the air raid shelter I found Granny cooking our tea. They had fires in there, and stoves, and we'd stay in there the whole evening and all through the night. Granny said, 'What do you want, love? Sausages and a baked potato?' I said: 'Yes. O. K.' We had a good time in the shelter. It was warm. We had sing-songs and bunks to sleep on. When a neighbour came in we welcomed them. Everybody was equal and pulled together. If somebody came into the shelter who we didn't know we said: 'Hello, love. Where do you come from?' We didn't turn anybody away. Sometimes during air raids the bombs came a bit *too* close and it got scary, but I don't think the shelter would have stopped a bomb from killing us if one had hit it. [14]

After Esther moved in with Granny Johnson they shared their rations, but Esther found a way to supplement them. Her relatives in British Guiana proved handy when she wrote to them and asked for help:

Times were hard during the war. Food was rationed. There was no fruit. Things were so bad they started selling whale meat, but I wouldn't eat it. I didn't like the look of it. We made a joke about it, singing Vera Lynn's famous song 'We'll Meet Again' with new words, 'Whale meat again!' Often Granny said: 'We could do with this, we could do with that.' So I wrote to my family in British Guiana and asked them if they could send us food. They were better off than us because the Americans were based there. Two weeks later a bloody great big box arrived. Everything was in it, all sorts of tinned food. After that I asked Granny: 'What grub do we need?' So I sent more lists. We welcomed those food parcels. [15]

In 1944 the Germans sent flying bombs over and they were known as doodlebugs. The engine had a low, humming sound. Pauline Henriques (see Chapter 3) described them as 'very alarming. I didn't like them at all [but] I couldn't bear going into the shelters. I couldn't stand it … I'd rather have the bombs.'[16] Esther recalled:

> When I heard it [the doodlebug] I knew I was safe, but when the engine stopped I wondered where it was going to drop. It was really frightening because they killed thousands of people and a lot of them dropped on Fulham. As soon as the engine cut out I'd say: 'Oh, God, it's stopped. Where am I going?' I'd lay down in the kerb or wherever I was and waited for it to explode. I'd just lay down and hope and pray it wasn't going to go off there.[17]

Air-raid wardens recorded that thirteen doodlebugs fell on Fulham between 18 June and 2 August 1944. Leslie Hasker in *Fulham in the Second World War* (1984) commented: 'The last of the flying-bombs in Fulham, and in fact the last incident in the Borough for the entire war, was at Beaumont Crescent at twenty minutes before midnight on Wednesday August 2. Seven people were killed and twenty-seven seriously injured. There was considerable damage.'[18] Esther remembered the incident, which she described as 'terrible' because it also demolished half of Dieppe Street which backed onto Beaumont Crescent:

> The air raid sirens warned us that doodlebugs were on their way so off we went to the shelter. We were waiting in the shelter for the all-clear when suddenly there was a terrific explosion and the shelter shook. A doodlebug had flattened parts of Beaumont Crescent and Dieppe Street! People were killed and many were left injured and homeless. Luckily our house was alright, even though it was number thirteen! We called it 'lucky thirteen' after that! At first the air raid warden wouldn't let us go back home because it wasn't safe. They'd hit the gas mains. So we all had to stay at the Lillie Road Rest Centre until it was safe to return to our homes.[19]

From 1941 the British government began to recruit service personnel and skilled workers in the British West Indies (see Chapter 6). They were recruited to come to the United Kingdom to work in factories and it has been estimated that about 2,500 were employed in war factories in the north-west of England. One of them was Esther's cousin Claude. He arrived in London from British Guiana and, on his way north, made an unexpected visit to his cousin:

One night he turned up on the doorstep. He said: 'I've come to see you. Can I stay for a few days?' He asked me to help him buy some tools that he needed for the factory work. Before he went up north, he told me he wanted to see a bit of London. So Granny and I gave him a bed. Granny's son, Charlie, who lived downstairs, came up to see us. He didn't know Claude and Claude didn't know him. Charlie shook his hand and said, 'How are you going, mate? You coming over the road for a drink?' That's the difference between people then and people today. Then Nell, who lived across the road, came over to me and said, 'Are we going to have a party for him, Esther?' So we had a party for him, but nobody knew him. They just wanted to welcome him because he was my cousin. In the old days people respected each other, and helped each other.[20]

Britain after the War

Friendly and outgoing, Esther found it easy to integrate into the multi-cultural Britain of the post-war years, but she was saddened by the Notting Hill race riots in 1958: 'It was a terrible time for black people. I didn't think anything like that would ever happen in this country.' Esther survived a war against Adolf Hitler and fascism; race-hating teddy boys in the 1950s; Enoch Powell's inflammatory and objectionable speeches on race in the 1960s; race-hating skinheads in the 1970s; and – one year before she died – the murder of Stephen Lawrence. She believed that 'if they'd stopped Enoch Powell and the National Front right at the beginning they wouldn't have got a hold'.

In 1991 the publication of Esther's life story, *Aunt Esther's Story*, co-authored with her adopted nephew Stephen Bourne (Granny Johnson's great-grandson), gave her a sense of pride and achievement towards the end of her life. Two years after she died a revised and updated edition of the book was published.

At the end of the war, Esther took Stephen Bourne's mother Kathy, aged 14, to see St Paul's Cathedral. Like so many others, Esther found it hard to believe that St Paul's had survived the German bombardment of London (the Blitz, doodlebugs and V-2 rockets). For many, including Esther, the beautiful and majestic cathedral symbolised the hope and strength of the British people. 'Look at St Paul's Cathedral,' Esther said to Kathy. 'There's not a mark on it. We're lucky. We've still got half a street, but some poor souls have ended up with nothing.'

CHAPTER 5

THE EVACUEE EXPERIENCE

On 1 September 1939, anticipating massive air raids, the British government began to evacuate schoolchildren and mothers with infants under 5 years old from threatened cities. Further waves of evacuation followed in 1940. The hallmarks of every small evacuee were a gas mask in its cardboard box and a luggage label giving the name of the child. Though many books and documentaries have been written and produced about Britain's 3.5 million evacuees, information about black evacuees is limited and hard to find. A rare example is Ben Wicks who, in his book *No Time to Wave Goodbye* (1988), acknowledged the existence of black evacuees but only fleetingly. He described John Jasper as one of five children in his family who were evacuated to Darwen in Lancashire. In a brief extract from their interview, Jasper described for Wicks his evacuation experience as a story of rags to riches. The vicarage where they stayed was 'like Buckingham Palace' and the children were taken on holidays to places like Blackpool and Wales where they stayed in four-star hotels: 'We lived in a lovely house just outside Preston with a farm and we were given a pony and a donkey. There were very few black people in Darwen and none at all outside Preston.'[1] It is frustrating that the author did not elaborate. He did not identify where John Jasper and his siblings came from, nor did he mention their parents. Ben Wicks didn't acknowledge how they felt about being black evacuees in a predominantly white community. Wicks may have conducted a more comprehensive interview with John Jasper but, if he did, little of it survived in the book. However, I later came across a photograph of five unidentified black evacuees in a 1940 edition of the BBC's Empire Service magazine *London Calling*.[2] The caption condescendingly describes the children as 'picaninnies'. A reference to Darwen identifies them as John Jasper and his siblings. Further investigation on the internet reveals that the Jasper children – Sidney, Tom, Florence,

Mary, John (born 1934) and Dorothy – all came from Manchester. Their parents, Tom (a ship's fireman, merchant service) and Dorothy, were married in Salford in 1924. At the time of writing, no further information about this family has been forthcoming.

Ben Wicks also mentions a small but revealing anecdote about two 'tiny black children', evacuees who were ignored in a school yard until 'a kind couple decided to give them a home'. A school teacher, quoted by Wicks, said 'imagine the surprise to the neighbourhood when their well-dressed parents turned up in a week's time with a carload of food and presents for the foster parents'.[3]

The two tiny black children were not alone in being ignored by potential foster parents. In some cases the problems experienced by black evacuees were reported to the League of Coloured Peoples (see Chapter 1) who did everything they could to help. In one of their early wartime newsletters, published in November 1939, one such case from Blackpool was reported:

> Among the large party of children which came to our district were two little coloured boys. Nobody wanted them. House after house refused to have them. Finally a very poor old lady of seventy years volunteered to care for them. She gave them a good supper, bathed them and put them to bed. As she folded their clothes she discovered two letters addressed to the person who adopted them. Each letter contained a five pound note.[4]

Deara Williams

In 1933 Deara Williams was born in Butetown, Cardiff, to an African father, Philpott Williams, and his African–Welsh wife, Kathleen. When Deara was a baby she was chosen to play Paul Robeson's daughter in the film *Sanders of the River* (1935). Her most memorable scene is the one in which the American star Nina Mae McKinney (playing her mother) sings her a lullaby. In 1940–41, when the Germans began bombing the Cardiff docks, Deara was among many Butetown children who had to be evacuated to places like Aberdare and Pontypridd. Local historian Neil M.C. Sinclair explains in *The Tiger Bay Story* (1993):

> Deara's back bedroom in Tiger Bay faced the rear of the houses in Bute Street. During the course of the war Gerry bombs eventually hit buildings in Bute Street and her whole back bedroom window was blown into the bedroom. The enormous blast caused absolute terror in poor Deara. Events like these led to the evacuation of the youth of the community.[5]

The Cozier Family

The strategic importance of the docks in Canning Town and Custom House in the East End made it one of London's most vulnerable areas. During the 1940–41 Blitz, the area became one of the most badly bombed parts of Britain. Many buildings used by the local black community were destroyed, including the Coloured People's Institute. To avoid the intensive bombing, Joseph Cozier from Canning Town was evacuated with his sister Joan and brother Christopher.

The Cozier family lived in Sandford Street in Canning Town. The head of the household, Joseph Cozier, was born in British Guiana and ran away to sea at the age of 14. He eventually settled in the growing black community of London's East End. A number of black families lived in the area around the Royal Group of Docks even before the First World War. These docks were the largest in the world and the Port of London was the most famous in the British Empire. Many black families settled in the streets around the 'sailortown' area of Victoria Dock Road which ran from west to east from Canning Town to Custom House. The number of African and Caribbean seamen who settled in the area increased during the First World War, which caused some resentment from the local white population. Situated off Victoria Dock Road, Crown Street was known locally as 'Draughtboard Alley' because black and white families lived side by side, but, in July 1917, the homes of black men in Crown Street were targeted and attacked by white gangs. After the end of the First World War, in August 1919, demobilisation and lack of employment led to further attacks on the families in Crown Street, but these were not on the same scale as those in Cardiff, Liverpool and other port towns.[6]

In 1920 Joseph Cozier married an Englishwoman, Florence Tindling, and they had eight children. Their eldest daughter Anita recalled that when she was growing up there were very few black women in their community: 'So black seamen married white women and quite a lot of mixed marriages turned out all right because they were good to each other. Where we lived there was no feeling that mixed marriages were wrong.'[7] Their son Christopher has described their father as a communist and:

> very educated. He could speak three languages ... he always found work. He took menial jobs on the railways. Dad was respected in our community. Everyone called him 'Mr Cozier'. All the old coloured men were respected and addressed as 'Mr'. White and black people respected each other. When I grew up in the 1930s, racial prejudice did not exist in our community.[8]

When the war started, Anita went to work in a sweet factory in Silvertown after leaving school at the age of 14. At the same time, 8-year-old Christopher was evacuated with his sister Joan (aged 12) and brother Joseph (aged 10) to Great Bedwin, near Marlborough in Wiltshire. Joseph takes up the story:

It was an experience I would never liked to have missed. We went with the school, St Joachims, a catholic school in Custom House. There was a crowd of us from the East End, but we were the only coloured children. We were given our gas masks and the whole school was taken on a coach to a railway station and then we went off to a village. It was quite an adventure because we'd never left home before. We were taken to the village hall in Great Bedwin where the vicar and some women from the village offered different children to villagers for fostering. Each child had its name called out and was told to stand on the stage. The villagers came and picked the children they wanted, but we were left out. They only picked the white children, except a little boy who had impetigo. Afterwards there was just Joan, Chris, myself and this boy with impetigo left in the village hall. I thought to myself, 'I won't let this bother me'. I was with my brother and sister anyway. At the end of the day the vicar took us to his vicar-age, but he wasn't married, and didn't have a clue how to look after us. So he asked one of our teachers to feed us. But she was a spinster and couldn't cook either. Instead she fed us garibaldi biscuits with milk and raisins for breakfast, dinner and tea! When the health visitor came, she told the vicar we must be given proper meals. Luckily for us, Mrs MacDonald, an Irish woman who had been evacuated to the same village with her two daughters, knew our family and took us under her wing. She was a lovely woman. She mended our clothes, and took us for walks in the countryside. We were together for about two years. I don't know what would have happened to us if she hadn't been there. We had the run of the vicarage, and access to orchards and forests. We even had a canal, something we'd never seen before. It was a very happy experience. We roamed all over the countryside. It was an adventure. There was always something new to find out every day. Mum and Dad visited us when they could, and Dad wrote us letters. Mum couldn't read or write. When we returned to London, we had great difficulties adjusting. We lived right on the docks. We could see the funnels of the ships at the top of our street.[9]

Kenny Lynch

Not all children were evacuated. Some stayed with their families because they were considered too young to leave or because their parents wanted to keep them close by. Kenneth 'Kenny' Lynch was also born in London's

East End, in 1938. His family lived in Cornwall Street, Stepney, and he was the youngest of thirteen children born to a Barbadian father, Oscar Lynch, a seaman who had served in the Merchant Navy during the First World War, and an English mother, Amelia. Kenny said he was too young to be evacuated and remained in London right through the war with his parents. He didn't get to know his older brothers and sisters until after the war:

> I didn't really know me brothers and sisters. I didn't know them until just after the war. They were evacuated to Llangefni in Anglesey, North Wales. I remember they all came back speaking with Welsh accents, which was quite funny. But I stayed behind with my mum and dad because you had to be older to be evacuated. I was only a year old when the war started. I just remember it being a very funny time. We used to go down these air-raid shelters every night, and we were bombed out of about three houses. We just used to move in with the person next door, or into one of the houses that was still standing. We must have moved about four or five times. I remember it as if it happened only yesterday. I can remember watching our house get bombed as the sirens went. We walked out of the house, got about four or five hundred yards away, and this great big flame went up. My old man said to me 'That's our house. So we'll probably move in with somebody else tomorrow'. And then we'd go down the shelter and everybody would be singing – as a kid growing up, I remember it as a great fun time. There weren't any other black families in Cornwall Street, and I don't remember seeing a lot of black people. I know that in the East End – places like Hackney and Poplar – there were blacks, but, as far as I can remember, I never saw that many. And I was a bit of a novelty. Being a cockney, I never had any trouble in those days, because there weren't many black people around. My father was from Barbados and had been here since he was sixteen. He was fifty-eight when I was born, which means he came to this country in the 1890s. He never lost his Barbadian accent – mind you, I couldn't understand a word he was saying half the time, even though he had been here quite a long time.[10]

Marie Kamara

Marie Kamara was 8 years old and living in Fulham, London, when she was evacuated in September 1939. She describes her mother as an unmarried middle-class black British lady of Ethiopian descent, and her grandfather as an Ethiopian who came to Britain in the 1920s and worked as a chef at one of the first Indian restaurants in London. She describes her family as 'the only black family in our neighbourhood but I didn't experience any problems; I had lots of friends, who were all white, and I wasn't aware that I was different or black'.[11]

Marie was evacuated to Winchester: 'Every child was taken in, one by one, and I was last. No one wanted to take a black child! But eventually a place was found.'[12] Marie was evacuated several times during the war and in 1944, when the doodlebugs started falling, she became very frightened and was sent to Mr and Mrs Venning, 'a very posh couple', in Penzance, Cornwall:

> I loved it there. I was very spoilt. Mr Venning ran a local shop. There was a maid called Muriel. On Thursdays Mrs Venning would go out, and then I was able to go into the kitchen and talk to Muriel, which I really enjoyed. They also had a farm, and we would visit at weekends and stay in a caravan. I really enjoyed being there. I saw lots of things grow and learnt a lot about nature. I was never made to feel different with that family. I remember listening to the radio during my evacuation, but to hear the BBC from London was painful for me because it made me miss home more. But I did like Alistair Cooke's *Letters from America*, that was great. I went to the local school. I was a lone evacuee, but I loved school, except for the time we did a play and I was made to black up, like the other children, as one of three golliwogs. I wasn't happy about that at all. I remember the song 'Jolly little golliwogs'. I was very upset about having my face blacked up! But I was always in the school plays; I enjoyed performing and did lots of plays and singing. After the war, when I was sixteen, I went into show business with my eldest sister, and I joined Britain's first black ballet company, *Ballet Negres*.[13]

Joan Lloyd-Evans

Only one black evacuee has ever been interviewed for a television documentary. On 3 September 1969, on the thirtieth anniversary of the outbreak of the Second World War, the BBC screened *Where Were You On the Day War Broke Out?* Among those interviewed was Joan Lloyd-Evans who, at the age of 4, had been sent from Liverpool to the safety of mid-Wales. She was also featured in an article in the *Radio Times*. In the documentary, an animated and bubbly Joan, who was fostered with her school friend Lily, reveals two incidents on her arrival in the Welsh village. The first was curiosity shown by a mother and her daughter to the 'coloured' arrival, and the second was her shock at meeting a cow for the first time. The latter was an experience common to many evacuees who had been raised in cities and were unfamiliar with the countryside:

So we walked up this main high road and all of a sudden this lady and this little girl stopped and they looked at me as if I was something from Mars because they'd never seen a coloured person before in their lives. And the lady said to the girl 'Would you like to go and touch the little coloured girl?' The little kid came over and rubbed my arm. So we went on walking and the lady in charge of us said 'Which field would you like to go through? The one with the cows or the ordinary one?' Lily said 'Let's go through the ordinary one' but I said 'No, let's go through the one with the cows in it!' But as we were coming towards the cows, one of them reared its head and went 'Moooooooo!' and I screamed. I was petrified![14]

CHAPTER 6

'FRONT-LINERS' IN CIVILIAN DEFENCE

In response to a manpower shortage, from 1941 the British government began to recruit skilled workers in the West Indies to work in the factories of the United Kingdom. It has been estimated that throughout the war around 2,500 were employed in war factories in the north-west or as foresters in Scotland.[1] The *News Letter* of the League of Coloured Peoples began reporting on their progress in March 1941: 'Fifty technicians arrived from Jamaica and disembarked at a Scottish port, whence they entrained for an English centre in the north, and are now hard at work in the factories there. The men were all in good health and spirit, and were met by Mr Ivor Cummings [see Chapter 2] who read to them the League's letter of welcome.'[2] A further report in the *News Letter* in November 1941 stated that 'three parties of West Indians numbering in all 188 men have been brought over to this country ... The Ministry of Labour is therefore particularly anxious through its Welfare Department to ensure that while these men are our guests they shall be made to feel in every way welcome in the United Kingdom both in the factories and in our ordinary communal life.'[3] The appointment of Learie Constantine as a welfare officer (see Chapter 2) to support the workers was regarded by the League as 'something of an inspiration'. In July 1942 the *News Letter* published a lengthy report describing a successful visit to London by a group of Liverpool-based Jamaican technicians. The League sponsored the visit which included trips to Oxford, Windsor, the Houses of Parliament and the Post Office, and a tour of London that included the Tower of London, St Paul's Cathedral and Madame Tussauds. On 20 June they attended a reception by the Rt Hon. Ernest Bevin, HM Secretary of State for Labour.[4]

In December 1941, soon after the arrival of the first groups of West Indian war workers, the United States entered the war. In the spring of 1942 the first black troops began to arrive in Britain, but the American army was then a 'Jim Crow' (racially segregated) army. Graham Smith, author of *When Jim Crow Met John Bull* (1987), a study of black American soldiers in Britain during the war, says: 'The problem of the West Indians soon became apparent, even before the first black Americans had arrived. Two white US marines assaulted a West Indian in London in March 1942 and the incident was reported to the Colonial Office.'[5]

'A Shameful Business': the Case of George Roberts

In 1944 the *Guardian* newspaper and the *News Letter* of the League of Coloured Peoples reported on an incident involving George Roberts, a West Indian electrician who had volunteered to come to Britain to support the war effort. His journey had taken him from his home in Antigua in the Caribbean to Liverpool in December 1942, where he took a job in a war factory. Roberts had been reported for failing to attend his Home Guard duties without reasonable excuse. Roberts had joined the factory as a volunteer, without compulsion, and he carried out his duties without incident until October 1943. He explained that he failed to attend his Home Guard duties because he had been refused admission to a dance hall on account of his colour. He had returned to the dance hall wearing his Home Guard uniform but had again been refused. Police at the entrance did not stop him but when he asked for a ticket he was told: 'Sorry, we cannot sell you a ticket because you are a coloured man.' On this particular night there were a lot of black American GIs about and the American military police were keeping them away from the dance hall.

Roberts was prosecuted for the offence of refusing to undertake his Home Guard duties and a fine of £5 was imposed. An appeal against the verdict was made, which was not heard until the quarter session of August 1944. Learie Constantine gave evidence on behalf of Roberts and described him as a 'very good character'. Roberts was represented by the defence barrister Rose Heilbron.[6] Mr Edward Hemmerde KC, the Liverpool Recorder and a former Liberal MP, denounced the 'colour bar' that Roberts had experienced. He was 'clearly outraged at Roberts' predicament, especially since technically he had broken the law and thus had to be fined. The Recorder like many others felt that during the current period of strife things should be different in Liverpool. There should be no discrimination, especially towards those who were aiding the war effort.'[7] Hemmerde reduced the fine imposed on Roberts to just 1 farthing.

Mr Hemmerde said: 'If anything that I may say may offend citizens of some other Allied countries, let me say that the Allied nations make up the democratic world, and if they have a colour prejudice they must occasionally come into collision with people who have not. I happen to be one who has not.' Giving judgement, Mr Hemmerde said:

> I do not understand how in the British Empire, with so many coloured people as its citizens, anything in the way of a colour bar can exist or ever be allowed to exist by any Government that is worth the name of Government. When people come here to risk their lives they are entitled to think that they are coming to conditions of decency and order in a country that claims the title of imperial in its best sense. If they find that a noisy and intolerant minority are not prepared to give them equal rights, I think they have a right to be angry. I think it is impertinence for any country to accept the aid of coloured people from any part of the world and then to say: 'Our laws don't enable us to deal with you on terms of complete equality' ... If you accept aid from coloured people you accept them, as your friends and as people whose aid you are proud to receive, and they should be the first to receive justice at your hands. But they do not receive it, and it is a shameful business. Mr Roberts is breaking the law, when, having come here to serve the country, he refuses to be insulted. The fact that he is guilty may be more the object of laughter than anything else ... We would like to remind all dance hall proprietors that discrimination against Negroes is exactly the same ... as Nazi discrimination against Jews. It is a very dangerous policy for them to pursue in Britain, law or no law.[8]

In August 1945 the League of Coloured Peoples' *News Letter* reported that Roberts, 'whose Home Guard case was given great publicity and called forth an historical comment from the Liverpool Recorder', had returned safely to his home in Antigua.[9]

Butetown

A good example of a culturally diverse community pulling together for the war effort is Butetown in Cardiff. Though not as badly hit by bombing as cities such as Swansea, Plymouth, London and Coventry, parts of Cardiff – including Butetown – sustained heavy bombing because of the docks and munitions factories. In 1942 the League of Coloured Peoples' *News Letter* acknowledged the work of Cardiff's 'coloured front liners': 'They have stood up to enemy action with courage and calmness. Many of the women are helpers at the Rest Centre and during a "blitz" in January last, helped to entertain and feed over three hundred and sixty people evacuated from their homes.'[10] However, in March 1944, at the League's annual general meeting, Robert Adams drew attention to the feeling of some black people in Cardiff who considered that the League 'catered only for students and coloured persons of standing'. Dr Moody said it was unfair for anyone to make such a charge against the League, particularly in Cardiff, where, when seamen had been denied their nationality in 1935, the League had carried out an investigation whereby the authorities had to recognise British colonial seamen.[11]

In his book *Negroes in Britain* (1948), Kenneth Little acknowledged that in some air-raid wardens' posts, 'on a minor scale, and with some different nationalities involved, an interesting illustration of international and inter-racial co-operation is afforded'.[12] Little was referring to the two air-raid wardens' posts in Cardiff: one at the Anglican church and the other at the Wesleyan Methodist church at the other end of the district. The latter's staff included a Maltese boarding-house keeper as sub-warden and a number of West Indian, West African, Arab and Jewish men and women as wardens and messengers. Little says: 'The A.R.P. duties in the district in general appear to have brought about quite a strong sense of comradeship and co-operation.'[13] In the Imperial War Museum there exists a Ministry of Information photo of Butetown's 'International Warden's Post' at work in 1943. The photo includes Edward Bovell who, in 1950, at the age of 84, was featured in A.L. Lloyd's *Picture Post* photo spread of Cardiff's dockland, 'Down the Bay'. Bovell was photographed by Bert Hardy, and Lloyd captioned the photo 'The Man With the Longest Memory in Butetown'. Bovell came to Cardiff from Barbados in 1885 and settled in Butetown's Sophia Street. He remembered the race riots of 1919 and long periods of unemployment after the First World War. He worked as a ship's cook until 1940 and then 'served as warden in local A.R.P. post comprising 14 nationalities'.[14] Further investigation reveals that Edward Bovell died in St David's Hospital, Cardiff, on 18 February 1961 at the age of 94. On his death certificate his occupation was given as 'Ships' Cook (Retired)'.

Sapper Box and 'The Suicide Squad'

Acts of bravery from black 'front-liners' were reported from the start of the war. In 1940, when a German delayed-action bomb was discovered buried in the garden of a Welsh town, a man was described in a *Daily Mirror* newspaper report as a 'West Indian coloured soldier'. He bravely dug down to the bomb and made it harmless. The soldier had undertaken similar tasks in France and he had volunteered for the hazardous operation. His commanding officer's permission was asked for and granted. Local people were moved away from the neighbourhood and the soldier, helped by comrades forming a 'suicide squad', dug a narrow hole 6ft deep. He was out of sight when he reached the bomb, which he made safe before bringing it to the surface. The people of the neighbourhood were so impressed with the soldier's act of bravery that they made a collection of £10 and presented it to him. He shared it with the comrades who helped him. A police officer who was standing near the scene of the operation told the *Daily Mirror*: 'The soldier had nerves of steel. He was as cool as if he was merely digging out a drain.' The report was acknowledged in the League of Coloured Peoples' *News Letter*.[15] When the League investigated the report the soldier was identified as Sapper E. Box. A letter from his commanding officer was published in the League's newsletter and explained:

> [Box] is a member of a section whose duty is to deal with unexploded bombs. On this particular occasion, he, together with the other men of his section, removed a bomb from a house and he then assisted his officer to remove the fuse and so render it harmless. Sapper Box is constantly engaged with the rest of his section on work of this nature, which is naturally of a highly dangerous nature, requiring the pluck and determination which it is clear that he possesses. The report you forward is highly picturesque, but without doubt Sapper Box, along with his comrades, is performing very excellent acts every day.[16]

'Front-liners'

The League of Coloured Peoples' wartime newsletters are an invaluable source of information about black civilian defence workers. After the Blitz started, the League began to publish reports about the contribution made by black citizens. For instance, in December 1940, A.A. Thompson, the Jamaican academic and general secretary of the League, praised the work of black 'front liners'. He said:

> In London especially one is amazed at the numbers of coloured men who have accommodated themselves to the novel circumstances of the war, and are to be found working ... as Wardens, A.F.S. [Auxiliary Fire Service] men, members of Stretcher Parties, First Aid units, and Mobile Canteens. One feels that the contribution these men are making to the defence of London ought to be given the fullest publicity.[17]

Thompson listed some of the black 'front liners' he encountered, though he is careful not to break wartime censorship by identifying their locations. He describes Mr Headley, a mining engineer from British Guiana, as 'the respected warden of an area that has repeatedly been bombed'. Mr G.A. Roberts of Trinidad, a member of the League's executive, 'is now ably serving the Auxiliary Fire Service'. Thompson describes 'Buzz' Barton as 'a well-known Jamaican boxer, now a First Aid worker in London'.[18] Granville 'Chick' Alexander, another eminent Jamaican, is 'now a member of a London First Aid Party'. Thompson adds that he has seen Alexander working at various bombed areas and also in a mobile canteen, 'and when I asked him whether he wouldn't prefer the peace and quietness of Jamaica, he replied, "Not likely! And miss all this fun?"' In his report, Thompson concludes that 'the contribution of the coloured population in proportion to its numbers is pretty considerable. This fact should be acknowledged.'

The London Blitz

There were occasional air raids on Britain in June, July and August 1940, but Hitler's blitzkrieg ('lightning war') began on London on 7 September 1940. The sustained bombing of London by Nazi Germany, known as the Blitz, continued until 10 May 1941. By the end of this period over 43,000 civilians had been killed and more than a million houses destroyed or damaged. Important munitions and shipbuilding areas were targeted. While the Germans never again managed to bomb London on such a large scale, they carried out smaller attacks throughout the war.

The first air raids of the Blitz on London were mainly aimed at the Port of London in the East End, causing severe damage, which the Germans hoped would create a division between those living there and the rest of London, but they did not succeed in this. From mid-September to mid-November raids took place day and night, and in October 1940 London experienced its worst air raid, when 400 German aircraft bombed the capital for six hours.

The civilians of London had an important role to play in the protection of their city. The main objective of Germany's leader was to destroy the morale of the civilian population, but he failed. Many people who were not willing or able to join the military became members of the Home Guard, the Air Raid Precautions Service, the Auxiliary Fire Service and many other organisations. Among those who became civilian defence workers in London at this time were Fernando Henriques, Jamaican-born but raised in a middle-class London suburb; E.I. Ekpenyon from Nigeria; and Len Bradbrook who was born in Lambeth.

Fernando Henriques (Fire Officer)

Fernando Henriques was born in Kingston, Jamaica, in 1916 and settled in London with his family when he was 3 years old. The story of his older sister Pauline is told in Chapter 3. Their father was a successful import and export merchant and wanted his six children to have an English education. Fernando was educated at a Catholic grammar school. When war was declared, Fernando's 'immediate reaction' was to join the armed forces:

> There was no thought that through my colour I would be thought to be outside the conflict. My experience at the recruiting centre in Central London was traumatic. An RAF sergeant told me quite bluntly that 'wogs', that is people of non-European descent, were not considered officer material. That of course was in 1939. A year later, as Britain became pressed, the situation became quite different. I cannot say that disgust invaded me totally at this rejection. It was rather like being confronted with hatred by someone you loved and thought loved you.[19]

Rejected by the RAF, Fernando decided to defend London in another capacity: 'I joined the National Fire Service in September 1939. I remained as a fireman for three years during which only one incident occurred which made me conscious of my colour. This was being told by an irascible officer that my quarters were too good for a "nigger".'[20] As a fireman during air raids, Fernando found himself constantly on the alert, but 'the Fire Service provided long periods of standing-by when I could study. This I did, and to the surprise of both my friends and myself obtained an Open Scholarship to Oxford.'[21] In 1944 Fernando became president of the Oxford Union and later a professor at Sussex University.

In the June 1941 edition of the League of Coloured Peoples' *News Letter*, Fernando highlighted the discrimination faced by some black men when they attempted to join the Air Raid Precautions Service. He described the experience of a friend who put his name down at the local town hall for enrolment as a full-time warden, only to be rejected when he attended the opening lecture for the warden's course. He demanded to see someone in authority but when he came face to face with the controller of the department he was told that there was no room for black people in the ARP. Aggrey House, a centre for colonial students set up by the government in Bloomsbury, London, took up the case and Fernando's friend received an apology from the controller. Fernando said: 'He is very happy in his job and has won the respect of both officers and men in his depot.'

In the same article, Fernando listed the names of some of the black ARP workers in the London area, and noted that St Pancras 'has a particularly strong coloured ARP section', including the following stretcher-bearers who all possessed the certificate of the St John's Ambulance Brigade: Chick Alexander and Sam Blake (Jamaica), Charles Allen and A.K. Lewis (Freetown, Sierra Leone), Laryea (Accra), Ote Johnson and A. Kester (Nigeria) and E. Gonzaley (Trinidad). He adds that D.E. Headley (British Guiana) was the head warden at St Pancras, G.A. Roberts (Trinidad) was a leading auxiliary in the AFS at the New Cross Fire Station, and Billy Williams (Sierra Leone) was a warden at St Marylebone:

> But the list is endless. Every London borough has at least one representative of the coloured population in London ... Coloured people as a whole have really come forward and shown their willingness to co-operate with the people of Britain in their titanic struggle. Despite all setbacks we are fighting in the front line, and will continue to do so. We are more than proud to say that the coloured population of London and Britain have come forward in this way.[22]

E.I. Ekpenyon (Air Raid Warden)

In his report for the League's *News Letter*, Fernando Henriques also mentioned E.I. Ekpenyon, a Nigerian from the town of Calabar who originally came to Britain to study law. He began training as a warden with the Air Raid Precautions Service as soon as the war broke out. As an air-raid warden in St Marylebone, Ekpenyon worked as an official in charge of local arrangements for air raids. He was responsible for running air-raid shelters, giving advice to his community, keeping lists of people living locally, helping with rescue work and warning people about the blackout (during the war all outside lights were switched off and people had to make sure that no lights could be seen from within their homes – hence people put up 'blackout' screens or curtains).

According to his daughter, Oku Ekpenyon, her father carried out his ARP duties conscientiously and she has described one event, during a night raid in the London Blitz, which always remained in his mind. Her father was standing on top of a 100-ft high building when he saw the sky light up with searchlights and heard the shells of anti-aircraft guns bursting as fires started in different parts of the city. Oku explains that, as a senior warden, her father regularly went out on patrols to ensure that the blackout was enforced and kept a 'census' of people in private and business premises – essential information when a building was bombed. She said:

He had a day and night off work each week but that did not stop people in his sector turning up on his doorstep if they needed him. My father's popularity locally showed the ambivalence that existed when he had problems with one of his shelters. The shelterers were of many different nationalities and beliefs. The bombing had forced them into one another's company, a situation that would never have happened in normal times.[23]

In a pamphlet published in 1943, *Some Experiences of an African Air Raid Warden*, Ekpenyon described how he challenged racism in the air-raid shelters:

Some of the shelterers told others to go back to their own countries, and some tried to practice segregation. So I told the people that though I am an air raid warden in London I am still an African. I said I would like to see a spirit of friendliness, co-operation and comradeship prevail at this very trying time in the history of the Empire. I further warned my audience that if what I had said was not going to be practised, I would advise those who did not agree to seek shelter somewhere else.

He added:

It amuses me to know that in the district where I work the people believe that because I am a man of colour I am a lucky omen. I had heard of such childish beliefs, but I am delighted that such beliefs exist, for wherever my duties take me the people listen to my instructions and orders, and are willing to allow me to lead them. So I am able to control them, which makes my duties lighter in these troublous days.[24]

During the war Ekpenyon made several broadcasts for BBC radio's Empire Service in *Calling West Africa*. In the first transmission on 11 July 1941 he described his duties as an air-raid warden, such as tackling the fires started by incendiary bombs, and recalled several frightening experiences during air raids. On one occasion he had to evacuate a shelter that had suffered bomb damage and, while helping an elderly lady to another shelter, another bomb came down. He threw her to the ground and protected her by lying on top of her.[25] Two years later, in his pamphlet, Ekpenyon elaborated on his experiences of air raids:

I found the shelter had been damaged and was in darkness, and about 120 people were in a state of confusion. As I was standing on the top of the stairs, I shone my torch on my face and signalled to them to be quiet. I managed to make myself heard, and told them plainly that if they wanted to be saved from fire they had to keep cool and take orders from me. Failing that, they and I would have to remain in the building and face our fate, which would be a very unpleasant one. The people became quiet and we were able to evacuate everyone … I had to carry a frightened woman from the damaged shelter. In the street the droning of the planes and the bursting shells increased her fright, so that she gripped me round the neck and I was nearly choked. I braced myself and carried her to a place of safety.[26]

In another BBC transmission, made on 18 July 1942, Ekpenyon described an event he had attended that June in the company of Sir Donald Cameron, the ex-governor general of Nigeria. They had visited a war factory and the visit was marked by the unveiling of the Katsina tank, built from funds raised in Nigeria. During lunch Ekpenyon was bombarded with questions about Africa.[27] Ekpenyon also appeared in a newsreel film made by the Colonial Film Unit that featured the Katsina tank, but sadly no prints of this film appear to have survived. After the war Ekpenyon hoped to resume his law studies but financial considerations forced him to work as a postman. In 1951 Ekpenyon died of heart failure at the age of 52.

Len Bradbrook (Civilian Defence Worker)

Len Bradbrook was born in Lambeth, London, in 1904 and became a popular figure in his local community.[28] Like with so many black people from the working classes who integrated into the wider, white community, information about Len is very sketchy. He was described in the book *A Century of Childhood* (1988) as 'one of the first black children to be brought up in Lambeth', and in a short interview in the book he said that 'the neighbours used to lift up the coping of the pram to have a look at me, because there were no black babies at that time in Lambeth'.[29]

It is known that he was prominently involved with the Lambeth Mission from the 1930s. He was recalled by a local resident, Daisy Moore, in 1993 as the 'black man' who, through the mission, ran the Ideal Cinema: 'He was the only black man we knew as kids. Kids used to pull his hair because they thought it was wool … But he was the superintendent there to us kids … he was a nice man. We never knew he was coloured – he was just Len Bradbrook to us kids. He used to run the Boys' Brigade and the Girls' Life Brigade.'[30] So far it has proved impossible to find more information about Len, but a clue to his war work can be found in the caption of a photograph that has survived in the Lambeth Archives. It reads: 'London Borough of Lambeth Light Defence group, c.1945.' Len has been identified as a member of the group of civilian defence workers.

Len Johnson (Manchester)

Len Johnson, known as Manchester's 'Uncrowned King of Boxing', was born in Manchester in 1902 of a West African father and an Irish-Mancunian mother.[31] In spite of being acknowledged as one of the finest middleweight boxers of the 1920s and 1930s, Johnson was prevented from fighting for British titles because he was black. His war service in civilian defence is briefly described by Michael Herbert in his biography *Never Counted Out!* (1992). From 22 December 1940, Manchester became the seventh most heavily bombed city in Britain during the war. At first Len worked as a rescue foreman, but he was later transferred to an ARP centre where he was a member of the heavy rescue squad. Contact with Mr Herbert has revealed some of the correspondence he received about Len's war work.

One correspondent, Miss I. Roach, recalled that when Len was in the 'Manchester Civil Defence' he worked in the rescue squad at the Park Street (West Garden) Depot where she was employed as an ambulance driver. Miss Roach describes Len as 'a smashing bloke, friendly with everyone, and liked by everyone'. Mrs M. Raine remembers that Len loved a game of billiards: 'He was a big man – very kind and gentle and perfectly mannered. We all respected him.' Another correspondent, Neville Robson, was struck by Len's 'gentlemanly demeanour, quite unexpected to me, for a boxer', and described Len's wartime role as a member of the civil defence heavy rescue squad based at the ARP centre in the old school on Claremont Road, Moss Side, in Manchester:

> My father was superintendent of that Depot and spoke very highly of Len's excellent record. The heavy rescue squad were equipped with mostly old single decker busses, painted grey and with all the old seats taken out, and windows boarded up. These were full of ropes, axes, crowbars, jacks, spades and other equipment and the job was to rescue folk trapped in their houses and other buildings after the bombings which were very heavy in Manchester. Liverpool suffered just as much. Dad used to tell me that Len would work as a 'human dynamo' and would not worry about the tremendous risks he was taking of the building collapsing onto him.

In 1943–44 Len worked as a civil defence instructor in the Civil Defence Reserve (Unit No 1) which was located at Kent's Bank, near Grange-over-Sands, Cumbria. These units were set up by the Ministry of Home Security to meet any unexpected attacks by the German Air Force. Len joined the unit in Cumbria as a specialist in first aid and physical training. However, his group officer, Mr A.C. Rowell, said that boxing was 'the one subject he never talked about [and] he never encouraged any young person to become interested in this subject'. Michael Herbert said: 'Obviously his years of training as a boxer and dealing with injuries sustained in the ring had given him a wealth of experience in this area … Len is remembered by other members of the unit as a very sociable person who was well respected by everyone.'[32]

CHAPTER 7

WHEN ADELAIDE HALL WENT TO WAR

Adelaide Hall's contribution to the British war effort is best summarised in a letter written by a fan, Mrs Florence Cross:

> During the war a party of us went to see her. Her performance was interrupted by the air raid siren. As we were ATS [Auxiliary Territorial Service, the women's branch of the army], from the gun site in Hyde Park, we stayed put as it was an unexpected night off. We thought we would wait till the show started again but it didn't stop. Adelaide sang and sang, the bombs dropped around us, and no one left. She was wonderful. I've never forgotten her.[1]

The Jazz Innovator and All-Round Entertainer

In the 1920s New York-born Adelaide Hall was the famous stage star who introduced the popular song *I Can't Give You Anything But Love* in the long-running Broadway revue *Blackbirds of 1928*.[2] At the same time she was a jazz innovator as important and influential as Louis Armstrong and Duke Ellington. They were part of the generation of African American singers and musicians that created the sound of jazz.[3] In 1927 Adelaide's wordless vocal on the recording of *Creole Love Call* with Duke Ellington was innovatory, using her voice as a pure jazz instrument. *Creole Love Call* is acknowledged as a landmark in jazz history. In the 1930s Adelaide became an international star with successful appearances in Europe, including her London debut at the Palladium in 1931. She was also a headliner at New York's famous Cotton

Club. Acknowledged as a highly respected trailblazer for black women, Adelaide projected a glamorous, sophisticated image.

In 1924 Adelaide married a Trinidadian seaman – and British subject – Bertram Hicks. He gave up his job in the navy to manage her career. However, when Bert accompanied Adelaide on tour, he impersonated a South American with a Spanish accent. He did this to avoid confrontations with white racists since the tours took them to the racially segregated states of America's Deep South. At Bert's insistence, the couple eventually relocated to Europe.

In Paris Adelaide and her husband found themselves embraced by Parisians who were well known for their acceptance of African Americans, especially those with connections to the world of jazz. The couple opened a popular nightclub which they named *La Grosse Pomme* (The Big Apple). It attracted such well-known patrons as Maurice Chevalier, Charles Boyer and Josephine Baker but, with the threat of war and the possibility of a German invasion, Adelaide and Bert looked towards London for a new home – and a new nightclub. They made the move at the start of 1939.

Settling in London

When Adelaide and Bert arrived in London they took over the Old Florida nightclub, which they relaunched as the New Florida. It was situated in Bruton Mews, close to Bond Street and Berkeley Square, where Adelaide had a small flat above the club and Bert had an office. Though primarily a private membership club for the armed services, Adelaide's appearances in the Florida's late-night revues attracted many stars of the day, including visiting Hollywood legends like Fred Astaire and Bob Hope, as well as members of the royal family.

Fela Sowande, the Nigerian pianist and composer, worked as Adelaide's accompanist. Adelaide described him as 'a nice pianist who was always properly dressed with his white tie and evening clothes. Fela was quiet and unassuming. He wore spectacles, and Bert said he looked more like a medical student than a musician!'[4] Sowande was a musician who combined the classical and the popular with astonishing versatility. In the 1930s he supported his music studies by accompanying jazz artistes like Adelaide. He then became the first African composer to successfully mix African and Western styles. In 1941, when Sowande joined the Royal Air Force, his career took a different direction. He was transferred to the Colonial Film Unit where he was appointed musical director. Sowande selected all the music used in the soundtrack of their films. On 8 January 1940 a Pathé newsreel captured

Adelaide and Sowande in a show at the New Florida. Though brief, this historic film now gives us a glimpse of the interior of Adelaide and Bert's popular nightclub, and of Adelaide herself entertaining her patrons.

Outbreak 1939

When Britain declared war on Germany, American citizens were advised by their government to return home, but Adelaide wanted to stay in Britain; a great risk with the threat of air raids. Adelaide explained that she remained in Britain because she was married to a British subject and refused to leave him. However, Bert tried to persuade his wife to return home to her mother in New York, but she said: 'I wanted to stay because I liked England and the people here were very good to me. They were very kind. I didn't want to desert them, or my husband. So I stayed.'[5]

The war had hardly started when Adelaide began entertaining the troops. On 17 October 1939 she starred in a variety concert at the RAF Station in Hendon. Other artistes on the bill included Will Hay, a famous comedy actor, who introduced the show. The BBC broadcast part of the show, which was the first wartime concert broadcast live on air. Part of the concert, including Adelaide and the O'Gorman Brothers, was filmed by British Paramount News and this newsreel has survived in the Imperial War Museum's collection. In the film Adelaide can be glimpsed enjoying herself onstage performing a sing-along number with the troops, *I'm Sending You the Siegfried Line to Hang Your Washing On*, a variation of the more famous wartime favourite *We're Gonna Hang Out the Washing on the Siegfried Line*.

Lewisham Hippodrome (1940)

Just before the start of the London Blitz, Adelaide topped the bill at the Lewisham Hippodrome in Catford, south London, with her piano accompanist Gerry Moore. On the evening of Monday 26 August 1940, in the middle of her act, the air-raid siren sounded but most of the audience remained seated. The air raid started and everyone in the theatre could hear the bombs falling. Though the building was strongly constructed, the sound of exploding bombs close by was clearly felt in the auditorium. Adelaide encouraged the nervous audience to join her in some community songs and later recalled: 'We – the performers and the audience – were told that no one could leave the theatre because it was too dangerous. Outside everything was burning. So, we had to just carry on and I managed to get the audience to join in many of the songs.'[6] *The Stage* newspaper noted that the evening's performance ended around 10.45 p.m. and after that, to help calm the audience while the raid continued, Gerry Moore started playing popular music and Adelaide began singing some numbers.[7] *The Kentish Mercury* reported on 30 August that:

> Miss Adelaide Hall did really wonderful work. She has given several 'turns' after the normal programme each night this week. On Monday night the normal programme finished at about 10.50pm and then an impromptu programme was given by Miss Adelaide Hall (12 to 14 songs) ... Members of the audience joined in and then there was a dance. 'We kept them amused,' said Mr Vincent, the manager, 'and I think they enjoyed it.' This procedure was followed on Tuesday and Wednesday nights, when again Miss Hall was the mainstay of the impromptu programmes. A few went home each night but the majority of the audience stayed.[8]

On the night of 26 August, for four hours, with bombs exploding outside the hippodrome, Adelaide helped to entertain the nervous audience until the all-clear sounded at 3.45 a.m. Later that day Gerry Moore commented that his fingers ached so much from playing that he could hardly move his hands. Though Adelaide could barely speak, in a defiant mood she returned to the stage of the hippodrome the following evening to perform her act as scheduled.

Singing for Morale

Throughout the war, in addition to variety tours, Adelaide entertained at anti-aircraft sites and in underground train stations, where members of the public had taken shelter from the bombing. She said:

> When we performed during air raids we learned to become philosophical about the dangers we were being exposed to. We'd just go anywhere – within reason. Sometimes I had to improvise, and sing without music, but it was a challenge – and so rewarding – to get all the people to sing with me. When we walked the streets and saw the devastation we became hardened. We didn't worry too much about the terrible risks we were taking because we wanted to keep up the morale of the forces and the public. Of course in situations like the one at Lewisham Hippodrome, or another, when I performed in Southampton and the whole front of the theatre was blown away – are a little different. Still, you get to the point, finally, when you say 'they're coming over again, let's try to carry on,' and we carried on to keep morale from becoming too low.[9]

An engagement to sing at an anti-aircraft site in Regent's Park was particularly frightening:

> The first time I played there an air raid started and, when the guns started blasting, I thought my head was going to be blown off when they opened up! I'd never heard such a loud bang-bang. I turned to my pianist and asked: 'Are you all right, Ron?' He looked terrified and said, very quietly: 'Just about.' I was singing at another anti-aircraft site in Green Park when we heard the air raid siren. They told me to keep on singing but to stop when I saw the red light. Then I had to run to the shelter. It was very scary. [10]

The Bombing of the New Florida Club (1940)

In October 1940, during the London Blitz, Adelaide had a premonition that the New Florida Club was going to be hit. She told everyone to leave the club before the raid started. Bert ignored his wife. He told her that if a bomb had his name on it, it would find him. He stayed but Adelaide took flight and travelled to their cottage in Redhill, Surrey, with her secretary. When the air-raid siren warned of an impending raid, Bert took refuge in the cellar with the nightwatchman. As the raid intensified, Bert and the nightwatchman became increasingly intoxicated and afterwards he told Adelaide that he couldn't remember anything about the club suffering a hit. Bert and the barman were saved because they had sheltered in the cellar. An entry in Adelaide's diary for 14 October confirms the incident: 'House bombed.' The bombing of the New Florida is also included in the air-raid warden's log which gives the time of the incident as 9.30, the type of bomb is described as a high explosive and the total number of casualties was ten. [11] After losing the New Florida Club, Adelaide worked almost non-stop for the remainder of the war. She broadened her appeal by broadcasting for the BBC and entertaining the troops and factory workers. In 1941 Adelaide was reported to be the highest-paid female entertainer in Britain. Audiences loved her because she provided not only glamour, but welcome relief from the miseries, hardships and terrors of war.

Adelaide joins ENSA

In 1943, when Adelaide joined the Entertainments National Service Association (ENSA), one of the first things she did was to have a uniform specially tailored for her by Madame Adele of Grosvenor Street. She said:

'Oh, it was smart! It was sand brown, with a lovely cap, and I had a shirt and tie too. It was a first class uniform but I couldn't stand the collar. It was very stiff.'[12] Adelaide loved the uniform, and wore it with pride whenever and wherever she could.

Adelaide was proud of the fact that she was one of the first entertainers to enter Germany before the war was over. She said:

> I travelled through Germany for ENSA, appearing in garrison theatres every-where. As the war drew to a close, I moved along with the troops and it was a very dangerous thing to do, but I didn't think about that. I just did what I had to do. I was on edge, and sometimes very frightened, but I persevered. It was hard work but I'm glad I went. I loved it. In the towns and cities we visited there was not a street in sight – nothing. They had all been razed to the ground, and people were putting up little boards, made from bits of wood, to identify the names of the streets that used to be there. Eventually we got to Berlin, and then we came all the way back! Sometimes we travelled in our jeeps across the fields in the dark. I had my own jeep and a driver. We arrived at the camp and the hall would be packed with soldiers. The door opened and the place was full of soldiers and smoke. I did my cabaret act and the boys had a ball. Sometimes we didn't have a stage so we had to improvise from the floor. At some of the concerts I sang to thousands of soldiers and it was so moving when they joined in. I shall never forget the time they sang 'Swing Low, Sweet Chariot' with me. They all had different voices. Some were baritones, others sang high, and it was a wonderful thing to hear. We were in Hamburg when we were notified that the war had ended.[13]

Adelaide was one of the first entertainers to arrive in Berlin to congratulate the troops after the city had been liberated. After the war Bert couldn't get her out of the uniform; he told his wife: 'The war is over now, Addie, you can let that uniform go!'

After the War

After the war Adelaide kept on working as an entertainer in Britain. In 1988, at the age of 86, there was a triumphant, sell-out return to New York when she performed in her one-woman show at the Weill Recital Room at Carnegie Hall. In 1989 a Channel 4 television documentary, *Sophisticated Lady*, captured her in concert at London's Riverside Studios. In 1991 she celebrated her 90th birthday by taking part in an all-star tribute at London's Queen Elizabeth Hall. Ann Mann said in her review in *The Stage* (14 November 1991): 'When

Hall appeared on stage at the end of the concert the crowd went wild ... Adelaide Hall's staying power, vivacity and sheer love of the business in which she works, is something which should act as a lesson to us all.' In 2002 Adelaide was recommended for an English Heritage Blue Plaque, partly for her war service, but she was rejected. A letter from the Blue Plaques secretary explained: 'The Panel concluded ... that Miss Hall was insufficiently well known today to justify a plaque.'[14]

CHAPTER 8

KEEPING THE
HOME FIRES BURNING:
ENTERTAINERS AND WORLD WAR TWO

Entertainers played a major role in raising morale during the Second World War. They made themselves accessible to the public, troops and munitions factory workers up and down the country. They joined ENSA, the Entertainments National Service Association, an organisation set up in 1939 to provide entertainment for British armed forces personnel. Many well-known stars performed for ENSA, including Gracie Fields, George Formby and Laurence Olivier. Entertainers also made themselves available to the American troops after the USA entered the war in December 1941. At the outbreak of hostilities, there were many black entertainers and musicians working in Britain. Some of them were British-born, others were American expatriates who could have returned to the USA but preferred to stay in their adopted homeland, and the rest had settled here from various islands in the Caribbean. By the outbreak of war, many of them had built up a strong relationship with the British public and some were household names. Among the most famous were Leslie Hutchinson (popularly known as 'Hutch'), Elisabeth Welch, Ken Johnson (popularly known as 'Snakehips') and Adelaide Hall (see Chapter 7). In addition to being associated with their appearances in classy West End nightclubs, such as the Café de Paris, the wider British public were familiar with the above-named stars through variety theatres, BBC radio, Radio Luxembourg and, from 1936, a new medium called television. They were also among the best-selling recording artistes of the day.

African American troops who were stationed in Britain from 1942 suffered appalling discrimination from fellow white Americans. This meant that black troops were often prevented from attending shows put on by British enter-tainers. In 1942 a small group of black entertainers welcomed opportunities to put on shows for some African American GIs and this was reported by the newspaper columnist Hannen Swaffer in the *Daily Herald* (16 September 1942): 'Already Ben Lyon and his associates – who in their spare time are running ENSA for the United States troops – have arranged special concerts for the coloured soldiers at which only Negroes – Turner Layton, Adelaide Hall, Scott and Whaley and Elisabeth Welch – perform. Sometimes the audi-ence contains as many as 3000 black troops!'

At the outbreak of hostilities these well-loved stars of British popular music and entertainment were more than willing to support the British war effort. However, there has been no formal recognition of their war work. Hutch's biographer, Charlotte Breese, acknowledged that Hutch worked hard for the British war effort, 'diverting hundreds of thousands of people nationwide, often spontaneously and without pay on top of an already gruelling schedule. He was angry that his efforts were never publicly honoured. He felt cheated and passed over, and believed that his colour caused his rejection.'[1]

Leslie 'Hutch' Hutchinson

In Britain in the 1930s the Grenada-born cabaret entertainer Leslie Hutchinson was popular with the high society world of nightclubs in London's West End.[2] Fellow cabaret star Elisabeth Welch described him as a very elegant gentleman who enjoyed flirting with the ladies: 'He dressed beautifully in Savile Row suits and carried himself as an Englishman. One of his trademarks was the white handkerchief in his left sleeve. He was a lovely person who put on airs, but we didn't mind because he was having fun as well. He gave the impression that he always woke up with a smile.'[3]

Leslie showed talent for playing the piano at an early age. After leaving school he joined the Civil Service but at the age of 16 Hutch, as he became known, left Grenada for New York. He later recalled that he arrived: 'with a few dollars and a lot of ambition. I became an elevator boy [but] in the winter of 1917 I was without a job and absolutely broke. So I offered my services as a pianist at private parties. And that's how it all started.'[4] After turning professional he left America for Paris where he met Cole Porter, the songwriter who was to become his friend and musical alter ego. Hutch became the best-known interpreter of Porter's songs and there was even a joke that said Hutch knew the lyrics before Porter had written them.

In 1927 Hutch was invited to Britain by the top theatre impresario C.B. Cochran. In addition to appearances in Cochran's West End revues, Hutch established himself as one of London's most popular cabaret entertainers, appearing in such society nightclubs as the Café de Paris, Café Anglais and Quaglino's. His trademark white handkerchief was used to mop his brow. Mostly Hutch associated with the upper classes and such friendships suggest a degree of social acceptance. This was often superficial, however, for black entertainers were rarely accepted as individuals. His biographer Charlotte Breese gave the following observation in the BBC Radio 2 profile *Salutations* (1993):

> Hutch was a remarkably elegant man. Outwardly he conformed entirely and he became part of the set that were his clients. He was certainly invited to their houses at weekends although of course it would have been different at official functions in London where he was still expected to enter by the tradesmen's entrance. For a man with as much pride as Hutch it must have been extraordinarily humiliating. He was a walking threat in a kind of way because he was so good-looking.[5]

It is interesting to compare Hutch with Paul Robeson, for they were two of the most famous black men living in Britain in the 1930s. Socially they were embraced by the upper classes, but politically they were worlds apart. Robeson eventually turned his back on the 'smart set', supported left-wing causes and acted in left-wing stage productions. Unlike Robeson, Hutch did not embrace politics, at least not publicly, or take artistic risks. He enjoyed the good life too much.

Hutch's popularity extended beyond London's West End when he became a top-of-the-bill attraction in variety theatres all over the country. He also had a reputation as a womaniser. Adelaide Hall remembered him as a 'smart cookie' who 'mixed with the society people, and he loved society ladies. He had a gang of them! Boy, boy, boy, it's a wonder he wasn't shot or killed!'[6]

Due to the fear of air raids, during the first two weeks of the war cinemas, theatres, dance halls and other places of public entertainment were closed, but this proved to be a temporary measure. There were no air raids during the first year of the war and gradually places of entertainment reopened for business. In the third week of the war, Hutch was seen in a variety show at the Birmingham Hippodrome. While Hutch's onstage contemporaries – with the Lord Chamberlain's permission – made fun of Hitler and other Nazi leaders, Hutch preferred to focus on what he did best: singing romantic songs. In her biography of Hutch, Charlotte Breese acknowledges that his wartime appearances were greatly appreciated by the British public, especially during air raids, and quotes a 'Manchester fan' who remembered: 'The bombing started during his performance, but Hutch just carried on playing the piano and singing, also mopping his brow as usual. He helped us to forget the Blitz for a while … Hutch was a real trouper.'[7] Hutch was indeed a 'real trouper'. In the middle of an appearance in Glasgow the air-raid siren sounded, but he just shrugged his shoulders, went on singing, and defiantly told the audience after the all-clear went 'Let's sing our answer to that' and sang *There'll Always be an England*.

In 1942 Hutch was featured in a West End revue called *Happidrome* at the Prince of Wales Theatre in Piccadilly. This was adapted from the much-loved radio comedy series. *The Stage* newspaper noted 'Hutch sings ballads with all his accustomed sincerity and effect'.[8] In 1943 C.B. Cochran invited Hutch to take part in *Seventy Years of Song*, an all-star gala at the Royal Albert Hall in aid of Toc H, an organisation which created new clubs worldwide for members of the United Nations Forces. Although Hutch was never given recognition for his contribution to the British war effort, his fans never forgot what he did for them. A Newcastle fan wrote to his biographer: 'Hutch and people like him gave of their very best. Morale was very important. You needed a song or a joke. You could only have a concert if it was for charity, that's why there were a lot of them … He transported us out of our world and into another where tomorrow would be better.'[9]

After the war Hutch's sophisticated style of cabaret performing, so popular in pre-war and wartime Britain, was no longer in fashion, and gradually his health began to decline. Hutch died on 18 August 1969. His obituarist in *The Times* noted his 'fanatical' devotion to cricket, and the singer and actress Jessie Matthews said that he personified the carefree charm of those years before the war.[10]

Elisabeth Welch

When Britain declared war on Germany, American citizens were advised by their government to return home, but the expatriate Elisabeth Welch had made London her home. She stayed because 'all my friends were here and I didn't want to leave them'. Elisabeth was born in New York but settled in London in 1933.[11] For six decades she was one of the most popular singers working in Britain and a permanent fixture on London's West End musical stage. At that time she was the most famous black woman in Britain and a sophisticated, stylish interpreter of popular songs. The British public were drawn to her beauty and elegance, and her soft, lovely voice. Elisabeth regarded herself as American by birth but English in thought and interest, and London was her home for seventy years. Her love affair with David Astor ended during the war when his formidable mother, Lady Nancy Astor, the Tory politician, expressed strong disapproval of her son's inter-racial affair.

When war broke out Elisabeth joined the first concert party to entertain the forces in Britain. In an unidentified press cutting in her scrapbook, she described that first concert (for the Royal Air Force):

A little hall was packed. Appearing that night were stars like Evelyn Laye, Frances Day and the Western Brothers. Oh, a terrific company. No theatre in the world could afford to hire the lot of us at once. What wonderful appreciation we got! What a thrill we got out of doing it for nothing! We couldn't help having lumps in our throats.

Before ENSA was formed, Elisabeth was happy to continue joining some of her show business pals to entertain the troops:

A lot of artists would call up friends and get parties together, sometimes with War Office permission. If we went out of London, transport was laid on for us. Wherever we went the boys were very pleased to see us. Sometimes they were a bit stunned, agog at who was up there on the stage in front of them – people like Vivien Leigh, Kay Hammond and Michael Wilding. Often we had no stage. I've been on a truck, with a terrible broken down piano, to sing to about six men on an Ack-Ack site in the middle of nowhere. I don't think they really wanted me to sing – though, as the piano was there, I did – they just wanted somebody to talk to. They were bored, lonely, and tense, waiting for enemy planes to come over.[12]

Throughout the war, in between many stage, film and radio engagements, Elisabeth busied herself by singing to troops and war workers, a job that took her to Royal Air Force hangars, army huts, factories and workshops all over the country. She also toured the provinces many times in variety shows: 'I spent a season at Blackpool and many weeks in Bristol when that lovely city was under fire. I played morning shows in Manchester at the Opera House during their terrible Blitz. I was under fire at Portsmouth, Cardiff, Liverpool, and Leeds, and was in London many times when the place was torn to bits.'[13] Elisabeth also took part in benefits to raise money for various causes. On 26 September 1941, the *Daily Mirror* reported: 'Orphan children of London Fire Service heroes will be helped by an all-star variety concert at the Piccadilly Theatre, at which over a dozen famous stars are to appear.' In addition to Elisabeth, the names listed in the programme included the cream of British theatre and variety: John Gielgud, Rex Harrison, Roger Livesey, Ursula Jeans, Noel Coward, Lilli Palmer, Diana Wynyard, Doris Hare, Emlyn Williams, Edith Evans, Vic Oliver, Tommy Trinder, Flanagan and Allen, and Debroy Somer's Band. Elisabeth also volunteered her services for

London's popular Stage Door Canteen, which was opened by Bing Crosby in Piccadilly on 31 August 1944. A report in the *Daily Express* (19 April 1945) claimed that Beatrice Lillie had made more appearances than any other star (twenty-two in just under a year); Elisabeth was ranked second with 'more than 20 appearances to her credit'.

In November 1942 Elisabeth received a telegram from the War Office asking if she would travel to Gibraltar to entertain the garrison there in an all-star revue called *Christmas Party*. Only *Swingtime Follies* and one other ENSA show had visited Gibraltar before them. *Christmas Party* was organised by Hugh 'Binkie' Beaumont of H.M. Tennant's, a management team that made sure its stars played troop shows. The company flew out to Gibraltar on 23 December 1942, and fifty years later Elisabeth recalled in the *Sunday Telegraph*:

> Well, what greater compliment could be asked of a foreigner than to join the company of people like Phyllis Stanley, Jeanne de Casalis, Dame Edith Evans, Beatrice Lillie, John Gielgud, and Michael Wilding! I was very proud, and grateful! We were asked by the War Office to go out to Gibraltar to entertain the troops. Not ENSA, but HM [His Majesty's] Government itself, the men with red braid on their caps. I felt very grand. We flew out in a Dutch plane with the windows all blacked out because we weren't supposed to see where we were going. We landed in Lisbon in what looked like a sea of swastikas. Because Portugal was neutral everyone stopped there for repairs and refuelling, and it was quite a shock to step out of the plane and see Nazi planes all round us. We girls gave our own brasshats a shock too. We were all three wearing trousers and they asked us frostily to change, which we did not.[14]

During their four-week stay the company performed fifty-six shows. Most of the shows were given in the island's Rock Theatre but others included one on board a ship to more than 2,000 men, two in the local hospitals, and some on board battleships and aircraft carriers. They also toured gun-sites, where they talked to the men. Most of the troops had been stationed in Gibraltar for two years and so were a responsive and grateful audience. Elisabeth commented: 'They were very emotional days, especially out there in Gibraltar where the boys were going to be killed and the ships to be sunk. It's hard to sing when your throat tightens up and you are fighting back tears.'[15] John Gielgud briefly described Elisabeth's memorable performance in the May 1943 edition of *Theatre Arts*: 'Elisabeth Welch sings "Prayer for Rain," "Begin the Beguine," and "Solomon," in a black dress against a white satin curtain, and you can hear a pin drop while she is singing, but when she has finished the thunder of applause can be heard in the street.'

After the war, Elisabeth reigned supreme in London's West End's revues and musicals, and in 1985 she won rave reviews for her performance in *Jerome Kern Goes to Hollywood*, a celebration of the composer Jerome Kern. In 1987 a documentary film called *Keeping Love Alive* captured her live perform-ance at London's Almeida Theatre at the age of 83. When Elisabeth died on 15 July 2003 at the age of 99, Miles Kreuger, president of the Institute of the American Musical, told the *Los Angeles Times* (19 July 2003): 'Elisabeth Welch wasn't just another singer; she was a cultural icon, like Ella Fitzgerald is to this country. She could do anything … with the most sweet and plaintive voice, and she had absolutely impeccable diction and taste. In a recording career that began in 1928 and lasted into the 1990s her voice was absolutely untouched by time.'

Ken 'Snakehips' Johnson

In the late 1930s the British public witnessed a meteoric rise to fame of the Guyanese dancer and bandleader Ken 'Snakehips' Johnson.[16] At first Ken and his West Indian Dance Orchestra were mainly known to the exclusive and fashionable elite of London who frequented sophisticated West End nightclubs. By the outbreak of war the general public were familiar with the orchestra's swing music. They had successfully broken through to the mainstream of British entertainment with their BBC radio broadcasts and appearances on the variety stage. In the early years of the war the orchestra, smartly dressed in white jackets, with the handsome, elegant Ken as their leader, provided a first-class act to the general public. In the world of music it was generally agreed that Ken was not a great musician, but he had the gift of imparting his terrific enthusiasm for swing music to both jazz enthusiasts and the general public.

Ken came from a middle-class background. His father, Dr Reginald Fitzherbert Johnson, was a prominent private medical practitioner and government medical officer of health. While still in his teens, Ken was sent to England to continue his education at a public school. From 1929 to 1931 he was a pupil at Sir William Borlase's Grammar School in Marlow, Buckinghamshire. He did well at his studies, played the violin in the school chapel and played for the school cricket and football teams. His full height of 6ft 4in made him an ideal choice as a goalkeeper. After leaving school he was supposed to study medicine but chose law instead. However, swing music was in his heart, though he originally entered the world of popular entertainment as a dancer. His main influence was the London-based African American cho-reographer and dance teacher Buddy Bradley, whose film work, especially the musicals of Jessie Matthews, earned him the title 'Britain's Busby Berkeley'.[17] It was through Bradley that Ken made his on-screen film debut as a dancer in a nightclub sequence of the musical *Oh Daddy!* (1934).

In 1934 Ken visited Harlem in New York where he saw the jazz giants Cab Calloway and Fletcher Henderson. This was a key element in Ken's desire to form his own swing band, even though his knowledge of music was limited. In Britain in 1936, 21-year-old Ken made his dream come true when he teamed up with the successful Jamaican trumpeter Leslie Thompson and launched a new swing band called the Emperors of Jazz. These were the players that started to change British music by introducing American-style swing for the first time. However, though Ken could dance, he had limited musical expertise. A colleague once commented: 'He couldn't tell a B flat from a pig's foot!' Leslie Thompson later described Ken as a charming and vivacious young man: 'I took a liking to him … We had Ken out front – he was a tall, lean fellow, and he could dance … Ken didn't know any music but he could wiggle and waggle himself to the time of the music, and so keep onlookers amused and interested. Somehow he got his name put out there on the posters … he was such a nice boy, but he wanted money, and he got led off without being aware of the consequences.'[18]

The band was soon recognised as one of the country's top swing groups and was one of the few at the time to include black musicians from Britain and the Caribbean. This was the intention of Leslie and Ken, who were aware of the discrimination encountered by black musicians in Britain. Among those recruited for the original line-up were the Cardiff-born Joe Deniz and several Jamaicans, including Yorke de Souza, Leslie 'Jiver' Hutchinson, Louis Stephenson and Bertie King. Other members included Wally Bowen, who originated from Trinidad, and Robert Mumford-Taylor, whose father was from West Africa.

The band enjoyed residencies at the Old Florida Club (1936–38), Willerby's (1939) and the Café de Paris (1939–41), situated at Coventry and Wardour streets. The Café de Paris opened its doors in 1924 and was one of the top nightspots in London. It featured an oval, mirrored room and a spacious dance floor, and attracted members of the royal family and aristocracy, as well as eminent political figures and stars of the silver screen. Elisabeth Welch, who made her London cabaret debut there in 1935, described the Café de Paris as 'the grand night club of London and all the big names of cabaret played there. It was very chic and very smart.'[19]

In 1937 Thompson quit the band following a dispute with Ken; he didn't believe a non-musician could lead the band. Nevertheless, Ken took over the leadership of the band and recruited several Trinidadian musicians, including Carl Barriteau, Dave 'Baba' Williams and George Roberts. He also enlisted

Dave Wilkins from Barbados. The band was renamed Ken Johnson and his West Indian Dance Orchestra. Elegant Ken projected an image of the gentleman about town and was likened to two famous and stylish American dancers: Fred Astaire and Bill 'Bojangles' Robinson. Under Ken's leadership, with his extra-long baton, the band became the toast of the West End and, because the Café was 'wired' for BBC radio broadcasts, the band's frequent appearances on the air waves helped to raise their profile with the British public.

Elaine Delmar, the daughter of band member Leslie 'Jiver' Hutchinson and goddaughter of Ken, later said the band was styled very much on the black American bands that had very showy elements: 'The guys were very elegant, often in tails, with carnations. They were turned out beautifully and of course Ken Johnson was a stunning looking guy and a dancer. There was nothing quite like them around at that time.'[20] Ken's main achievement was to provide a positive image for black musicians in Britain and to show that Britain could produce a black bandleader as sensational as African Americans like Cab Calloway and Duke Ellington. Everyone who met Ken commented on how kind and gentle he was. He always found something nice to say about everyone. Outside of music he loved good food, wines and, above all, a cigar. Sailing was one of his favourite pastimes.

The Café de Paris, situated underground directly beneath the Rialto Cinema on Coventry Street, was thought to be impregnable. It was advertised by its owner, Martin Poulsen, as 'the safest and gayest restaurant in town – even in air raids. Twenty feet below ground.' Poulsen deluded the public into thinking there were four solid storeys of masonry above. In his history of the Café, Charles Graves said: 'all that protected the Café from a direct hit were the glass roof of the Rialto Cinema and the ceiling of the Café de Paris itself.'[21]

At 9.30 p.m. on Saturday 8 March 1941, Ken was having drinks with some friends at the Embassy Club before his show at the Café, which was not far away. An air raid was raging and no taxi was available. His friends begged him to stay, but Ken was determined to arrive on time for his appearance. He ran all the way from the Embassy Club to the Café de Paris, through the blackout and the falling bombs. He arrived at 9.45 p.m. but five minutes later two high-explosive bombs crashed onto the dance floor and one exploded in front of the bandstand. Charles Graves described the devastation: 'There was a flash like the fusing of a gigantic electric cable. All the lights went out. Masonry and lumps of plaster could be heard crashing to the ground.'[22] Band member Joe Deniz was there. He later recalled that the band had just started playing their signature tune, *Oh Johnny*, when the glass ceiling of the club shattered:

As we started to play there was an awful thud, and all the lights went out. The ceiling fell in and the plaster came pouring down. People were yelling. A stick of bombs went right across Leicester Square, through the Café de Paris, and further up to Dean Street. The next thing I remember was being in a small van which had been converted into an ambulance. Then someone came to me and said: 'Joe, Ken's dead.' It broke me up.[23]

Jazz historian Val Wilmer has described how Ken looked after the incident:

on the floor, close to the microphone through which he had introduced 'Oh Johnny', his red carnation still in the buttonhole of his immaculate tailcoat, without a mark on his body, lay the leader of the band, whose initials were emblazoned on the heavy music-stands which lay shattered and askew in the wreckage: Ken 'Snakehips' Johnson, 26 years old, had reached the end of a meteoric career.[24]

Reports of the numbers of dead and injured have varied, but most reports agree that over thirty people lost their lives that night at the Café de Paris, including its owner, Martin Poulsen. Another casualty was the Trinidadian band member, saxophonist Dave 'Baba' Williams. He had been cut in half by the blast. Yorke de Souza later recalled the shock and horror he felt when he found him: 'In the half-light I saw a body lying face downwards. [Dave] Wilkins and I tried to lift him up but the top of his body came away in our hands. It was Dave Williams. I felt violently sick as I let go of him.'[25]

Sixty others were seriously injured by the blast and in the aftermath looters 'prowled around the floor of the shattered nightclub, ripping open handbags, tearing rings off the hands of the dead and the unconscious. There was an epidemic of looting during the blitz, so serious that Scotland Yard set up a special squad to deal with it.'[26] In *The People's War* (1969) Angus Calder described the macabre scenes 'among the most indelibly horrifying of the period'.[27]

The publishing of the incident in newspapers was delayed because there were strict government restrictions on the reporting of air-raid casualties in wartime Britain. Newspapers were expected to maintain a balance between news and keeping up the morale of the public. At first the incident at the Café de Paris was played down and it took time for the facts, including the tragic death of Ken, to be made known. Some early press reports gave a clue to the location in London by the song title, *Oh Johnny*. Everyone associated this song with Ken and his orchestra; it was their 'theme' song. If readers knew this, they could probably work out which nightclub had been hit.

On 15 March 1941 Ken's death made front-page news in *The Melody Maker*.

The Nazi murder raids on civilians in London have caused the dance band profession to suffer some grievous blows, and it is the mournful task of the

'Melody Maker' this week to record the passing of some famous figures in the business who have fallen victims to enemy action. First and foremost is Ken Johnson, leader of the West Indian Orchestra, and one of the most progressive disciples of modern swing in this country.

Ken was survived by his mother in British Guiana. Following his funeral, she gave consent for his ashes to remain in Britain. Arrangements for Ken's final resting place were made by Ivor Cummings, an assistant welfare officer from the Colonial Office (see Chapter 2). Cummings, who had been a friend of Ken's, then contacted the headmaster of Ken's former school and requested permission for the ashes to be interred in the school's chapel. On 8 March 1942, one year after he was killed, Ken's ashes were interred during a memorial service at the chapel and the suggested order of service included the following hymns: *City of God, Through the Night of Doubt and Sorrow* and *What Sweet of Life Endureth*.

Britain's first black swing band was no more, and its surviving members went their separate ways. While he was alive, Ken Johnson's fame only lasted a few years, but he made a big impact on the British public, who mourned his tragic death during the Blitz. The fact that his name is still remembered by older generations is a testament to his legendary status in British show business.[28]

CHAPTER 9

LONDON CALLING:
THE BBC IN WARTIME

During the war the British Broadcasting Corporation, popularly known as the BBC, provided both news and entertainment for its listeners at home and overseas. After launching its radio service in 1922, the BBC gained a reputation for being stuffy and old-fashioned. Elisabeth Welch (see Chapter 8) described the BBC as 'Auntie' because it had a reputation for being prim and prissy.[1] In spite of this image, in the 1920s and 1930s the BBC was not an exclusively white organisation. Though black personnel would not be found *behind* the microphone as programme makers, a number of black singers and musicians enjoyed a high profile on BBC radio and – from 1936 to 1939 – the BBC's pre-war television service. For example, as early as 1934, Elisabeth Welch was prominently featured in the radio series *Soft Lights and Sweet Music* and, in 1937, at the height of his popularity in Britain, Paul Robeson was voted the most popular singer on BBC radio. In the series *The American Half-Hour* (1935) Alistair Cooke devoted a programme to 'the Negro'. The *Radio Times* promised that the programme would look at the Negro 'as orator, poet, preacher, writer, composer, and singer'. Poetry was represented by James Weldon Johnson and music by Duke Ellington and W.C. Handy. In 1939 the bandleader Ken 'Snakehips' Johnson (see Chapter 8) presented a programme about black Caribbean music called *Calypso and other West Indian Music*. Shortly after the war broke out, Elisabeth Welch was heard in another series, *Rhapsody in Black* (1940), in which she was featured with the black British contralto Evelyn Dove.[2]

During the war, black female vocalists like Elisabeth Welch, Evelyn Dove, Ida Shepley and Adelaide Hall (see Chapter 7) were regularly employed by the BBC in music and variety programmes such as *Monday Night at Eight*,

Variety Bandbox, *Starlight* and *Workers' Playtime* and, on the Empire Service, *Calling the West Indies* and *Calling West Africa*. In 1943 Adelaide was given her own series, *Wrapped in Velvet*. In May 1945, during the Victory in Europe celebrations, the African American entertainer Josephine Baker visited London and took part in several victory shows and BBC broadcasts. In fact, throughout the war, black musicians and entertainers could be heard in a range of morale-boosting music shows. BBC radio also launched the British career of the Trinidadian folk singer (and hero) Edric Connor.

Edric Connor

In the 1930s Edric Connor worked as a mechanical engineer, while in his spare time he researched and studied Caribbean folk music.[3] He was also a trained baritone. During the early part of the war he worked on the construction of the American naval air base in Trinidad and saved enough money to travel to Britain. He left Trinidad in December 1943 and on his arrival in London, in February 1944, he took a job working in a munitions factory in the East End, machining breech blocks for 3-inch guns: 'Although I had been away from lathes and milling machines for many years, it took me only five minutes to recapture my touch.'[4] Edric didn't stay at the factory for very long. He had already presented a series about Caribbean folk music on Radio Trinidad, and on his journey to Britain he carried with him some notes on this topic, including calypso, as well as letters of introduction to the BBC. Two weeks after his arrival he made his debut on BBC radio in *Calling the West Indies* for the Empire Service. However, a close call with a V-2 rocket almost ended Edric's career before it began. In December 1944 he left his lodgings in Ilford, Essex, and 'Five minutes later the explosion of a rocket occurred somewhere over Upminster. I began to count slowly. One. Two. Three. And the most awful explosion roared … The house swayed. The blast ripped the glass from all the windows. All the pictures left the walls. My bed was in another corner of the room. The rocket dug a thirty-foot crater just at the point where I would have been had I gone for my exercise. Thirteen people were killed in the houses nearby. Five of them could not be identified. I would have disappeared without trace.'[5]

Edric was also featured in another BBC series broadcast on their Empire Service, *Travellers' Tales*, and he played Joe in the musical *Show Boat* (Home Service, 24 July 1944), in which he sang the Paul Robeson favourite *Old Man River*. He also took part in *Tribute to the King* with a group of representatives of the British Commonwealth and Empire. This was broadcast immediately before King George VI's speech on VE Day, 8 May 1945. Edric's appealing voice and charming personality made a deep impression on listeners, and his widow Pearl, also from Trinidad, recalled in 1993:

> Towards the end of the war, and immediately after, the British government made an effort to show some appreciation for all the people from the colonies who had contributed to the war effort. Those little Caribbean islands had all stuck their necks on the block. Some of our young men had gone and died. My own brother joined the Royal Air Force and flew a Lancaster bomber. So the British government wanted to show some appreciation. There was an open-door policy. They weren't locking us out yet. But it didn't last. The BBC was also interested in helping to promote and assist some of the third-world people, and the Caribbean people. So Edric came to Britain at a good time. Doors were open to him. He didn't have to kick too hard.[6]

In the early post-war years Edric became a major celebrity on BBC radio and television, and a much-loved and respected ambassador for the arts and culture of the Caribbean.

The Man Who Went to War (1944)

A landmark year for black actors in BBC radio was 1944. In addition to Edric Connor's appearance in *Show Boat*, the Guyanese actor Robert Adams took leading roles in Eugene O'Neill's *The Emperor Jones* (20 May), and in a *Children's Hour* presentation he portrayed the African American leader *Booker T. Washington* (10 December). Elisabeth Welch starred in a dramatisation of George Bernard Shaw's short story *The Adventures of the Black Girl in Her Search for God* (19 June). However, one of the most innovative drama productions broadcast on BBC radio in 1944 was *The Man Who Went to War*.

Three of America's most famous black actors, Canada Lee, Paul Robeson and Ethel Waters, participated in this historic BBC radio production, which they recorded in New York. It was a rare opportunity for Ethel Waters, a star of musical theatre and cinema, to play a dramatic role. Paul Robeson had based himself in Britain from 1928 (when he appeared in the London stage version of *Show Boat*) to the outbreak of the Second World War in 1939, when he returned to America with his family. Throughout his British career Robeson frequently appeared on radio programmes broadcast by the BBC. He took part as the speaker of the prologue in *The Man Who Went to War*, this now forgotten – and lost – BBC 'ballad-opera' by the African American writer Langston Hughes. It was first broadcast in America on 20 February 1944, and then in Britain on 6 March (from recordings of the American broadcast). Robeson turned down the lead, Johnny Lee, because he was then appearing on Broadway in *Othello* and he was concerned about straining his voice. This part was taken by Canada Lee. Ethel Waters was cast as Johnny's wife, Sally. Inexplicably, this landmark production has never been mentioned in any of the numerous books about Robeson. The cast were brought together in New York by one of the BBC's top radio producers, D.G. Bridson, and he invited Langston Hughes to write the script. The following extract, taken from Bridson's autobiography, gives us some insight into the significance of this forgotten production which brought together some of the most important African Americans of wartime America:

My plan was to write a simple sort of folk-tale round the lives of a man and his wife in a town like London during the war. But though their story would be London's own, the town itself – like the man and his wife – would not be English, but Negro. The man joins up and goes to fight the war with his friends; his wife goes to work in a war factory and suffers all the terrors of the Blitz … The impact of the work in performance was incredibly moving. Ethel Waters' parting from her husband and her singing of *Sometimes I feel like a motherless child* almost stopped the show in the studio. The performances of Canada Lee and Paul Robeson, the rousing songs in the troop-train, *We're gonna move into Germany* and *Keep your hand on the gun*, the eerie spiritual *City called Heaven* sung in the air-raid shelter as the bombs came whistling and crashing down … As a gesture of friendship from one people to another, *The Man Who Went to War* was probably unique. As a prophetic echo of the Negro's post-war struggle for Civil Rights, it might have been a timely warning. Either way, it was quite one of the most popular broadcasts I ever had on the air, being heard in Britain by nearly ten million listeners on its first transmission alone.[7]

Bridson explains in his autobiography that the recording made by the BBC was promptly destroyed after its second broadcast in Britain 'by some fool of a BBC administrator'. It was many years later that the only surviving discs were discovered in America. They were taken into the BBC's New York office for copying onto tape that could be sent to Bridson in London. Instead of being copied, the actual discs were freighted to Bridson and – as the programme had been recorded onto fragile wartime stock (cut on a glass base) – they reached him in a thousand fragments, and that was the end of *The Man Who Went to War*.

But not quite. The Langston Hughes Estate has given permission for a short extract from the surviving script to be included in this book. In the air-raid scene Langston Hughes effectively captures the tension, fear, helplessness

1. Dr Harold Moody. See Chapter 1.
Courtesy of the Moody family.

2. Lilian Bader. See Chapter 3.
Courtesy of the Imperial War
Museum, HU53753.

3. African seamen outside West Indies House, a hostel opened in 1942 in North Shields by Harold Macmillan MP. See Chapter 2. Courtesy of the Imperial War Museum, D5765.

4. Learie Constantine introduces a group of West Indian workers to Ernest Bevin, the Minister for Labour, in London (1942). See Chapter 2. Courtesy of the Imperial War Museum, SG8615C.

5. Homeless people from London's East End, including a black mother and her child, after an air raid in September 1940. Source unknown.

6. Unidentified evacuee leaving London for the country (1940). See Chapter 5. Courtesy of the Imperial War Museum, HU55936.

7. From left to right: Kathy Joyce, Esther Bruce, Granny Johnson and Michael Joyce smiling through the Blitz. See Chapter 4. Author's collection.

8. Unidentified evacuees arriving in Eastbourne in September 1939. See Chapter 5. Courtesy of Popperfoto.

9. A group of African American GIs meet a policeman somewhere in England. Source unknown.

10. Elisabeth Welch signs an autograph at a concert for the troops somewhere in London. See Chapter 8. Author's collection.

11. From left to right: Hall Johnson, Josh White, Paul Robeson, Ethel Waters, Canada Lee and D.G. Bridson in New York at the recording of the BBC's *The Man Who Went to War*. See Chapter 9. Courtesy of the BBC/Redferns Music Picture Library.

12. Una Marson and Learie Constantine broadcasting for the BBC's Empire Service in *Calling the West Indies* (1942). See Chapter 9. Courtesy of the BBC.

13. Paul Robeson in *The Proud Valley* (1940). See Chapter 10. Author's collection.

14. Ken Johnson. See Chapter 8.
Courtesy of Peter Powell and
Andrew Simons.

Una Marson interviewing Ken Johnson, celebrated West Indian dance-band leader, in a BBC head-quarters studio. Una Marson is a well-known West Indian journalist who frequently takes part in our programmes. On Thursday of this week she will interview Rudolph Dunbar's Negro Choir in 'West Indian Starlight' at 6.15 p.m. EST (23.15 GMT)

15. Ken Johnson and Una Marson
broadcasting for the BBC's Empire
Service in 1940. See Chapter 8.
Source: *London Calling*, No 71,
9–15 February 1941.

16. A mobile canteen bought by the people of British Guiana and stationed at Chelmsford in Essex. The canteen travels to local districts feeding civil defence workers and the homeless after air raids. See Chapter 11. Courtesy of the Imperial War Museum, D3528.

17. The people of Jamaica supplied a Crusader tank to Britain. See Chapter 11. Courtesy of the Imperial War Museum, P1013.

18. Princess Omo-Oba Adenrele Ademola (Nurse Ademola) at Guy's Hospital. See Chapter 10. Courtesy of the Imperial War Museum.

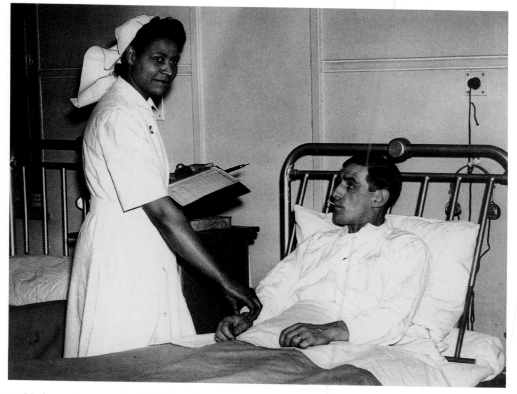

19. Under a scheme run by the Colonial Office, nurses from the West Indies underwent training at a London hospital. Nurse Monica Munroe from Grenada is seen taking a patient's temperature in Fulham Hospital. See Chapter 3. Courtesy of the Imperial War Museum, PL9610F.

20. Alvin Christie, from Jamaica, at work in the machine shop of a northern tank factory. See Chapter 6. Courtesy of the Imperial War Museum, D6202.

21. Constantine Higgins, a technician from Jamaica, is seen fitting a wheel to a tank in a factory in the north of England. See Chapter 6. Courtesy of the Imperial War Museum, D6210.

22. Munitions factory workers in the north-west of England listen to a variety programme broadcast by the BBC. See Chapter 6. Source: *London Calling*, No 151, 30 August–5 September 1942.

23. Colonel Charles Arundel Moody. See Chapter 1. Courtesy of the Moody family.

24. Len Bradbrook (front row centre, wearing beret) and members of the Lambeth Civil Defence Service (Light Rescue Party). See Chapter 6. Courtesy of Lambeth Archives.

25. Pauline Henriques. See Chapter 3. Courtesy of Biff Crabbe.

26. Esther Bruce. See Chapter 4. Author's collection.

27. Adelaide Hall. See Chapter 7. Courtesy of Iain Cameron Williams and Kate Greer.

28. A black prisoner of war in Nazi Germany. See Postscript. Source unknown.

29. Edward Bovell and members of Butetown's International Air Raid Warden's Post in 1943. See Chapter 6. Courtesy of the Imperial War Museum, D15328.

30. Fernando Henriques (top row, with the beard) and members of the Auxiliary Fire Service (AFS) in London, ready for action. See Chapter 6. Courtesy of the Imperial War Museum, D5544.

31. 'Keep Smiling Through – Black Londoners on the Home Front 1939–1945' exhibition at the Cuming Museum (2008). Courtesy of the Cuming Museum.

32. Adelaide Hall display (Keep Smiling Through). Courtesy of Andrew Warrington.

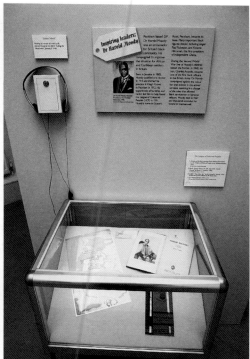

33. Dr Harold Moody display (Keep Smiling Through). Courtesy of the Cuming Museum.

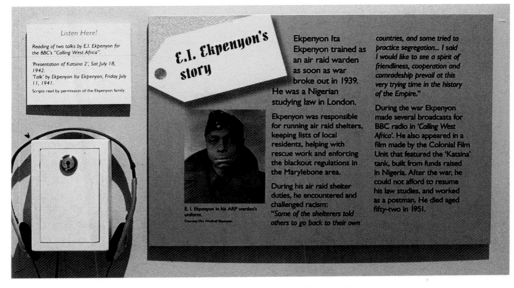

34. E.I. Ekpenyon's story (Keep Smiling Through). Courtesy of Andrew Warrington.

35. Esther Bruce's story (Keep Smiling Through). Courtesy of Andrew Warrington.

36. Help West Africa to Work for Victory (Keep Smiling Through). Courtesy of Andrew Warrington.

37. Ken Johnson and Elisabeth Welch display (Keep Smiling Through). Courtesy of the Cuming Museum.

38. Help the West Indies to Work for Victory (Keep Smiling Through). Courtesy of Andrew Warrington.

and community spirit experienced by those under fire on the home front in Britain. The cast featured in this sequence included Ethel Waters as Sally, Osceola Archer as Mrs Johnson, Cherokee Thornton as Grandpa, Theodora Smith as Lottie, William Johnson as Jerry and Melvin Green as the warden:

MRS JOHNSON: Sounds like a heavy raid doesn't it? I thought they'd be over again tonight.

SALLY: They always come when it's a full moon.

GRANDPA: Danged old planes – and me down here in the shelter helpless as a cooter. I'd like to fill them full of buckshot.

SALLY: All right Grandpa. You save your breath.

WHISTLE OF BOMB FALLING: EXPLOSION.

LOTTIE: (SOBS) Oh, why don't they go away? Night after night they come back.

SALLY: There, there, honey. Don't you cry, now. Crying won't keep them away. Try and go to sleep, then you won't hear them.

LOTTIE: (STILL SOBBING) I can't go to sleep. I've not slept since we were bombed out. I'm scared.

SALLY: Shhh! Don't take on so, honey! You'll make yourself sick.

LOTTIE: (SOBS) If it'd been your house they'd hit. I was trying to go to sleep when the bomb came ... I didn't know. (BREAKS DOWN)

MRS JOHNSON: We know, honey – but you're here now, ain't you? Safe and sound!

LOTTIE: (SOBS) I want my Joe.

SALLY: You mustn't talk about it now! Not now! You'll frighten the children, darlin'.

LOTTIE: (SOBS) I'm sorry, Sally. I'll try not to.

WHISTLE OF ANOTHER BOMB.

JERRY: Mama! Mama! Maybe that hit *our* house.

SALLY: We don't know what it hit, son.

GRANDPA: Now, Jerry. You keep quiet, like a man. Baby isn't crying.

JERRY: Baby don't know what it's all about. I do. I wish I had a gun, too.

GRANDPA: Now, if *I'd* got a gun – would I be here down in the shelter?

BEHIND SPEECH THE HALL JOHNSON CHOIR VERY QUIETLY HAS BEGUN TO SING 'CITY CALLED HEAVEN.'

SALLY: Grandpa, will you stop talking about guns. There's enough noise already.

LOTTIE: (NOT CRYING ANYMORE) It makes you feel so helpless. Just sitting here, waiting and listening. That's the way it was that night.

SALLY: Sshh, Lottie. Don't listen to the planes, honey. Everything'll be alright.

THE CHOIR NOW DROWNS THE QUIET CHATTER OF THE CROWD.

ABOVE THE SONG THE ALL CLEAR SOUNDS. DURING THE LAST LINE THEY BREAK IT UP TO SHOUT.

VOICES: There's the warden. Let the warden through. There's the all clear.

WARDEN: That's the all-clear going now. Grandpa! Sally! I've bad news for you.

SALLY: For us?

WARDEN: Yes, I'm sorry for you. Your house has been hit.

SALLY: Our house has been hit. What happened?

WARDEN: It just isn't there anymore.

JERRY: Mama, our house isn't there anymore?

WARDEN: No, sonny, it isn't there anymore.

GRANDPA: You mean – we've not got a home, now?

SALLY: (BEGINS TO CRY) Where shall we go? What shall we do?

MRS JOHNSON: Now honey, you ain't alone! I ain't been your neighbour all these years for nothing, living just down the street from you. Bring your children and Grandpa, and you come to live with us until you get straight. That is, if I still got a house. Warden, have I still got a house?

WARDEN: Yes, Mrs Johnson, your home is o.k.

MRS JOHNSON: Then come along home with me, honey, come on.

Una Marson and *Calling the West Indies*

The BBC Empire Service, which has been known as the BBC World Service since 1965, began in December 1932. Its broadcasts were mainly aimed at English speakers in the outposts of the British Empire, or, as King George V put it in the first royal Christmas message, the 'men and women, so cut off by the snow, the desert, or the sea, that only voices out of the air can reach them'. Radio came to the British Caribbean in the 1930s and the war helped develop radio broadcasting in the region. It was used to relay news of the war and to boost morale. Those radio stations relied heavily on the United States' radio networks or the BBC for news and entertainment programmes. The BBC's Empire Service helped enormously in this respect, with programmes like *Calling the West Indies* proving very successful.

One of the most influential black people at the BBC in wartime was the Jamaican feminist, poet, playwright and social activist Una Marson.[8] In the 1920s and 1930s there were few openings for Una to expand as a dramatist and playwright in Jamaica. She wanted to spread her wings and come to England, which she did in 1932. She was helped by Dr Harold Moody (see Chapter 1) and his family. Dr Moody gave her lodgings in his home in Peckham, as well as a job. For several years she worked as secretary to the League of Coloured Peoples, the organisation founded by Dr Moody. Before long she became well known in London as a feminist activist who would campaign on black women's issues, such as discrimination in the nursing profession.

In the BBC radio documentary *Voice – The Una Marson Story* (2003), Una's biographer, Delia Jarrett-Macauley, explained that she was initially drawn to Una through her poetry:

> I found a black poet and in some ways her poetry was helpful as it gave me an insight into her emotional life which I wouldn't otherwise have had access to, but also the poetry told me another story because many of her poems were about the experience of arriving in England, of quite bitter racial experiences. To hear her voice in poems such as 'Little Brown Girl' I get a sense of somebody who is searching, on a quest, but at the same time shocked to see how other people view her, asking questions, not only of herself, but also of a population of which she's now a member. Una Marson was one of the very first people in the Caribbean to start writing poetry in Jamaican patois, but that wasn't the only way in which she was experimenting in verse. Being in London meant having more contact with a range of artists including the Harlem Renaissance poets, people such as Eric Walrond, and reading work of Langston Hughes and Countee Cullen. And so Una also started to mix up the rhythms and she wrote some blues poetry such as 'Brown Bay Blues'.[9]

After spending some time in Jamaica, towards the end of 1938 Una found a new London home in the leafy suburb of Hampstead. In 1939 she accepted an offer from Cecil Madden, a BBC producer, to undertake some freelance work on his popular television magazine show, *Picture Page*. This work gave Una a stepping stone into the organisation. The outbreak of war on 3 September 1939 then gave her the opportunity to work for BBC radio and consequently she became the corporation's first black woman programme maker and presenter. Una's pioneering work for BBC radio spanned just over five years, from April 1940 to December 1945. During a trial period, Una took part in broadcasts about West Indians and the war effort, including *The Empire at War* (1 April 1940). She ended one of these broadcasts with the following morale-boosting statement: 'I am trying to keep the flag flying for dear old Jamaica in my own way here.'[10]

On 3 March 1941 Una was appointed as a full-time programme assistant on the BBC's Empire Service. In April 1941 an article in *London Calling*, described as 'the overseas journal of the British Broadcasting Corporation', announced Una's appointment as a member of staff. It described her background and brought home to overseas readers the realities of wartime London, and how it was impacting on the broadcaster: 'She has had the experience of having her house fired by one of Hitler's incendiary bombs, and her spare time is taken up as an air-raid shelter marshal in Hampstead.'[11] Her appointment coincided with the extension of the Empire Service to the West Indies.[12]

Through the weekly series *Calling the West Indies*, Una was able to send messages from servicemen and women in England to their families and friends in the West Indies. Listeners throughout the Caribbean would gather in front of their radios, sometimes up to three times a week, and wait to hear the Jamaican presenter say: 'Hello, West Indies. This is Una Marson.' In spite of the air raids and other wartime dangers, Una and her guests broadcast from a BBC studio and, although it was dangerous, Una understood the importance and value of *Calling the West Indies*.

In addition to her work at the BBC, Una took care of many West Indians, providing accommodation in her home as well as using it as a meeting place where they could get together and socialise. Erika Smilowitz says: 'Her crowded flat in Bayswater became a meeting spot for West Indian servicemen stationed all over England ... Always there was Una's sense of humour dominating the party; she loved to talk and laugh.'[13] Una was very conscious of the struggles faced by West Indians in Britain at that time, and on radio she 'had a knack of infusing her broadcasts with the personal as well as having a sense of the literary and the cultural'.[14]

Throughout the war, various editions of *London Calling* published photographs of Una with some of her guests, including Ken 'Snakehips' Johnson (February 1941), some Jamaican airmen (August 1941), a group of West Indian servicemen and women (December 1941) and Learie Constantine (August 1942). The pages of programme listings in *London Calling* offered limited information about the content of the *Calling the West Indies* broadcasts, but occasionally details were published.

The primary function of *Calling the West Indies* was to enable West Indian servicemen and women to send messages home to their family and friends, but from some of the information given in *London Calling* it is possible to appreciate the range and diversity of subjects offered to listeners. For example, the trade unionist Vic Feather gave a talk on trade unions (9 July 1942); there was a programme of songs and music by the black Edwardian composer Samuel Coleridge-Taylor (3 September 1942); greetings from West Indian foresters (then working in Scotland) (8 September 1942); hymn singing by a Welsh choir (21 March 1943); a programme of West Indian poetry, stories and songs presented by Una Marson (1 January 1943); Una Marson interviewing the Jamaican-born sculptor Ronald Moody (brother of Dr Harold Moody) who had escaped to Britain from Nazi-occupied Europe (1 February 1943); music from Band of the Grenadier Guards (9 September 1943); and a talk by Fernando Henriques (see Chapter 6) on 'The London Theatre Today' (7 November 1943). *West Indian Christmas Party*, 'a programme of greetings and entertainment', was broadcast on 26 December 1944 and featured singers Edric Connor and Ida Shepley, as well as groups of students and servicemen and women from Jamaica, St Lucia, British Guiana, Montserrat and Trinidad. In 1942–43 the Guyanese barrister and journalist Ernest Eytle read the news.

Towards the end of 1942 Una took part in George Orwell's series *Voice*. This enabled poets and novelists to read their work straight into the microphone. Consequently, Una devised her own literary series, clearly based on Orwell's format, and in 1943 she transformed a segment of *Calling the West Indies* into *Caribbean Voices*, a programme that was influential in shaping the future of the literary development of the Caribbean. *Caribbean Voices* proved to be a landmark series because at that time very few poets and playwrights from the West Indies had been published. The series gave them opportunities to raise their profile – and earn some money. The series is now recognised as the single most important literary catalyst for both creative and critical writings in the Caribbean. It ran from 1943 to 1958. In the West Indies the school curriculum was British and so students studied the work of Shakespeare, Dickens, Keats and Yeats. No West Indian writers were acknowledged and no one was encouraged to write in Jamaican patois. *Caribbean Voices* helped to change this.[15]

In 1943 Una made an appearance in the short documentary film *West Indies Calling*. Widely respected in wartime Britain, she counted the great literary giants George Orwell and T.S. Eliot among her BBC colleagues. Her international circle included prominent African Americans, such as the writers Langston Hughes and James Weldon Johnson. After the war Una continued to work in politics, broadcasting and literature until her premature death in 1965 in Kingston, Jamaica, from a heart attack. In 1998 Delia Jarrett-Macauley published a critically acclaimed biography, *The Life of Una Marson 1905–1965*, and in 2009 a Southwark Council Blue Plaque was unveiled by Delia on Una's former home in Brunswick Square, south-east London.

Delia says that the 'racial isolation, pride and wartime zeal which characterise Una's war poems would not have been the qualities the BBC was seeking. "Convoy" is a narrative poem describing a walk during which she sees a truck convoy, lets it pass and observes that every man on board waves to her.'[16] Every man on board who waves to Una is black. 'The Convoy' was published in the April 1945 issue of the League of Coloured Peoples' *News Letter*.[17]

The Convoy

Then each driver turned to greet me
As his truck went roaring by,
Brightly smiled or waiving gaily
As he quickly caught my eye.

There I stood, moved, yet unmoving,
Weeping with no sign of tears,
Greeting all these unknown soldiers
I had known a thousand years.

For they were my own blood brothers,
Brown like me, as warm of heart,
And their souls were glad to greet me
In the great white busy mart.

Our gay hearts grown sad and wiser
Stirred to life a second then,
A thousand words unsaid, were spoken –
And we each took heart again.

Oh my brothers, in the conflict
Of our own bewildered life,
How much strength we bring each other,
What fine courage for the strife.

The Colour Bar

During the war a discussion programme about racism in Britain was made but never broadcast. It was hosted by the anthropologist Kenneth Little.[18] The broadcast was called *The Colour Bar*, and three black guests openly discussed their experiences of racism. The guests were Aduke Alakija, a West African who was studying social science at Cambridge University; community leader Dr Harold Moody; and the actor Robert Adams. In the recording that was made in June 1942, the guests highlighted the mistreatment many Africans and West Indians faced when they arrived in Britain. Some encountered problems in finding accommodation, and Adams emphasised that 'colour prejudice is fairly general in this country'. After listening to the recording, G.R. Barnes, the BBC's director of talks, recommended that *The Colour Bar* be broadcast in the evening but suggested that the peak listening time of 9.20 p.m. be avoided for fear of 'exacerbating an already heated issue'. Barnes noted that the programme should be considered 'a conversation between friends'. However, during a weekly meeting with the Colonial Office, it became apparent that there had been an increasing number of complaints from black people about racism and discrimination in wartime Britain. The Colonial Office looked favourably on *The Colour Bar* and hoped that it would bring 'the whole subject [of race] out into the light of day'. Then Barnes had a change of heart. He was concerned that a discussion programme about racism 'was apt to deal in generalities and abstract questions which were often beyond ordinary men and women' in Britain. He recommended to the Home Service that they do not broadcast the programme. He 'very much regretted the decision' and insisted that the guests receive payment for their contributions. He also requested that the script be filed 'in case usage could be made of it at a later date'.[19]

Very little attention has been given to the black presence in BBC radio since broadcasting began in this country in 1922, and yet there is a rich source of black British history to be unearthed from the archives of the BBC. Some, but, regrettably, not many, of the programmes have survived. However, a large proportion of them exist in script form. This chapter can only highlight a little of this exciting 'hidden history', based on my own personal research. It is not meant to be exhaustive. Funding is needed the for the compilation of a comprehensive database of the numerous black broadcasters who participated in the early, formative years of BBC radio from the 1920s to the 1970s.

CHAPTER 10

FRONT-LINE FILMS

Cinema played an important role during the Second World War. In addition to films being produced for morale-boosting entertainment, there were films made for propaganda and shown at home and in the colonies. More work needs to be undertaken to fully acknowledge how black citizens of the British Empire were depicted in films in wartime, but this chapter will highlight how commercial and propaganda films created a space for them: whether they be newsreels, popular commercial feature films like *The Proud Valley* or the output of the Colonial Film Unit.

Ras Prince Monolulu

One of the first black people to be seen in British cinemas in wartime was Ras Prince Monolulu, the flamboyant racing tipster – and showman – a popular figure in the 1920s and 1930s.[1] Almost everyone in Britain had heard about him, and he couldn't be mistaken with his headdress of ostrich feathers, multicoloured cloak and gaiters, tartan shawl wrapped around his waist, a huge shooting stick-cum-umbrella in his hand and a lion-claw necklace round his neck. Then there was his catchphrase, 'I gotta horse!' which he shouted at the top of his voice. In the 1930s Monolulu, Leslie 'Hutch' Hutchinson and Paul Robeson were among the most famous black men in Britain.

One week after the outbreak of war, Monolulu was seen in the newsreel *London Carries On* (British Movietone News, 11 September 1939). The film's commentator, Leslie Mitchell, informed cinema audiences that Monolulu had 'evidently adapted himself to the new conditions'. Monolulu is seen amongst a London crowd, promoting gas masks and adapting his famous catchphrase to 'I gotta gas mask to protect you!' He adds: 'Are we afraid of Hitler? Are we downhearted?' To which the cheerful but determined crowd replies: 'No!' The film is in keeping with the spirit of the times. The war had just been declared and morale-boosting propaganda was needed, with Monolulu providing a reassuring figure. A few years later Monolulu was briefly seen in another wartime newsreel, *Children at St Pancras Station* (production company unknown, 10 July 1944), in which he talked to a group of child evacuees leaving London because of the bombardment of flying bombs (doodlebugs). Then there was *Peace on Earth* (production company unknown, 1945), in which thousands of Londoners are seen celebrating the end of the war outside Buckingham Palace. One of the happy faces is Monolulu's.

Paul Robeson and *The Proud Valley* (1940)

In the 1930s the charismatic African American Paul Robeson was the first black actor to attain stardom in British cinema. Though he disowned his first British film, Alexander Korda's *Sanders of the River* (1935), for its imperialism, Robeson found British film makers more accommodating than those in Hollywood. Films like *Song of Freedom* (1936), *King Solomon's Mines* (1937) and *Jericho* (1937) helped establish Robeson as a box office attraction, but he described *The Proud Valley* as 'the one film I could be proud of having played in'. However, he returned to America at the outbreak of the Second World War, thus ending his British movie career.

The script for *The Proud Valley*, written by the left-wing Herbert Marshall and his wife Alfredda Brilliant, enabled Robeson to express his socialist beliefs and portray the struggles of the working-class people of South Wales. For Robeson, making *The Proud Valley* was a rewarding experience both on and off camera. His biographer, Marie Seton, described how the Welsh people embraced Robeson and took him to their hearts: 'They knew he was a great singer. That meant a lot to them for music was as deep a part of their heritage as it was of his; but it seemed they found something else in him: the decency and simplicity of their own folk.'[2]

War broke out in the middle of filming and Ealing closed down the production for a couple of days. As an American citizen, Robeson could have packed his bags and departed for America with his family there and then, but he was committed to the film. When filming resumed, he remained in Britain until *The Proud Valley* was completed. In a memoir of his father, *The Undiscovered Paul Robeson*, Paul Robeson Jr recalls how his parents coped: 'Essie [his mother] drove Paul for the thirty-minute trip back and forth to the studio. The exercise became quite a problem when Paul had to work late, since the blackout rules often forced Essie to drive home in almost pitch darkness. Somehow, she always managed.'[3]

The Proud Valley was completed on 25 September and three days later Paul and Essie saw a rough cut of the film. The Robesons were thrilled, and on 30 September they boarded the USS *Washington* at Southampton for the journey home to New York. On 25 February 1940 *The Proud Valley* became the first film to be premiered on radio. That evening the BBC broadcast a sixty-minute version of the film, reproduced from its soundtrack, on their Home Service.

The closure of film studios and the dramatic fall in film production during the war years made it almost impossible for black artistes to work in the medium. Only a select few appeared, and these were mostly singers or musicians in featured roles in musical sequences of feature films or shorts, such as Cyril Blake in *At the Havana* (1940); Don Marino Barretto's band in *Under Your Hat* (1940); Adelaide Hall in Alexander Korda's *The Thief of Bagdad* (1940); the Jamaican baritone Uriel Porter in *He Found a Star* (1941); Elisabeth Welch in *This Was Paris* and *Alibi* (both 1942) and *Fiddlers Three* (1944); and Leslie 'Hutch' Hutchinson in *Happidrome* (1943). Films with a wartime setting, such as Noel Coward's critically acclaimed and Oscar-winning *In Which We Serve* (1942), failed to acknowledge the existence of black service personnel, but in the melodrama *2,000 Women* (1944) a small group of black women and children can be glimpsed among the female inmates of a German internment camp in France. (But if you blink you'll miss them!)

Towards the end of the war, the Nigerian character actor Orlando Martins played Jeremiah, an African freedom fighter, in *The Man from Morocco* (1945). The film told the story of a group of men of all nationalities who join the International Brigade in 1937 to fight against Franco and fascism in Spain. Peter Noble, in *The Negro in Films* (1948), said: '[Jeremiah] was shown to be a courageous fighter, an intelligent speaker and a good friend; he has a number of important scenes with the Czech captain, played by Anton Walbrook, and in every way is treated as an honoured member of a gallant body. Nowhere is there any reference to his colour, or any sort of discrimination indicated.'[4]

Welcome to Britain (1943)

The large numbers of African American GIs in wartime Britain drew attention to the escalating problem of racist attacks upon them – and some black Britons, Africans and West Indians – from white American GIs. In *Black and White – The Negro and English Society 1555–1945* (1973), James Walvin said that the problem became so widespread by the autumn of 1942:

that the Labour M.P. Tom Driberg questioned the Prime Minister about 'the introduction in some parts of Britain of discrimination against negro troops'. Churchill refused to be drawn on the issue, pointing out that the Minister of Information had already put on record the government's opposition to any form of discrimination. At its most blatant, discrimination consisted of open refusal to serve Negroes in public places. Such refusals became commonplace … Nor were such rebuffs the preserve of American Negroes.[5]

Consequently, a documentary film called *Welcome to Britain* was commissioned by the War Office from the Ministry of Information to address this problem. It was then handed over to the American Office of War Information for distribution amongst American troops. Released in December 1943, *Welcome to Britain*, devised and directed by one of Britain's most respected film makers, Anthony Asquith, was intended as a 'guide' to British behaviour for newly arrived American troops stationed in the UK.

The American actor Burgess Meredith, then a captain in the American army, acted as the film's on-screen guide and narrator. The purpose of the film was to show American GIs how to get along with the British people. In one sequence the comedian Bob Hope 'explains' the British currency system. Graham Smith says in *When Jim Crow Met John Bull* (1987): 'It included a quite remarkable sequence on race, asking the American soldiers to respect the different attitudes they would find in Britain. In effect the film granted the request that [John L.] Keith of the Colonial Office, amongst others, had wanted all along – the right to inform the Americans of the British view on this matter.'[6]

In *Welcome to Britain* Burgess Meredith shares a railway carriage compartment with an elderly English woman and a black soldier called Corporal Collier. The woman and the GI discover they are both from places called Birmingham – one in England and the other in Alabama. On leaving the train the woman invites both soldiers to tea if they are ever in *her* Birmingham. At this point Meredith speaks directly to the camera and informs white GIs that:

> there are less social restrictions in this country … You heard an Englishwoman asking a coloured boy to tea. She was polite about it and he was polite about it. Now … look; that might not happen at home but the point is, we're not at home, and the point is too, if we bring a lot of prejudice here what are we gonna do about 'em?

The script gave the impression that racial segregation in America would not change after the war, but:

nevertheless these were at this point frank words on race relations coming indirectly as they did from a ministry which had been a party to previous government statements of a very different nature ... The film was well received by those British critics who managed to see it, and General Lee's statement, encouraging US soldiers to take a fresh look at their racist attitudes, was especially commended. There was also extreme irony in the situation. Here was a British Government department (the Ministry of Information) which had in 1942 contributed to a policy encouraging the British to respect segregation because that was the American way, making a film the following year, with American actors and senior American staff officers, encouraging the Americans to respect racial integration in Britain because that was the British way![7]

West Indies Calling (1943)

West Indies Calling was a short, fourteen-minute documentary film made by the independent producer Paul Rotha for the Ministry of Information (MOI).[8] During the Second World War, the Films Division of the MOI was responsible for film propaganda in Britain. They assumed control of the GPO Film Unit (renamed the Crown Film Unit) for the production of official documentaries. Rotha's film showed how West Indians in Britain were involved in the war effort. It featured the Jamaican broadcaster Una Marson (see Chapter 9) at the BBC's Broadcasting House studio in London, hosting a broadcast to the Caribbean with two Trinidadians, Learie Constantine (see Chapter 2) and Flying Officer Ulric Cross.[9] They describe to listeners of Calling the West Indies, the popular BBC radio series, how people from the Caribbean are supporting the war effort. Constantine speaks about factory workers, and introduces some war workers, including Cross, a bomber navigator. Cross tells of his work in the RAF and speaks about some of the 10,000 volunteers for the armed services from the Caribbean. Representing 900 lumberjacks, Carlton Fairweather talks about forestry work by lumbermen from British Honduras. Although the introductions and commentaries sound stilted at times, the film footage that accompanies it provides some rare screen images of black participation in the Second World War. These include service personnel such as fighter pilots, engineers, factory workers, lumberjacks and nurses. The film ends with a dance in a BBC studio and much emphasis is given to co-operation between peoples of different national and racial backgrounds.

West Indies Calling was one of the few wartime films that depicted black people supporting the British home front, but it had a limited release. However, it has since reached a much wider audience with a video distribution in the

1990s by the Imperial War Museum in their education pack 'Together', inclusion in the BFI Mediatheque's *Black Britain* collection (launched in October 2007) and a DVD release. It is described by Wendy Webster in *Englishness and Empire 1939–1965* (2005) as 'an important film for any account of representations of the British home front, since it disrupted the boundaries between empire and metropolis where "home" was shown as white'.[10] Webster acknowledged that the film takes care to show the culturally diverse West Indian identity: white-Caribbeans, Indo-Caribbeans and African-Caribbeans: 'But the film is dominated by black West Indians who tell a narrative of both a "people's war" and a "people's empire" and insert themselves into this narrative ... [it] shows Britain as a decent and tolerant nation.'[11]

Colonial Film Unit

The Colonial Film Unit (CFU) was a documentary production company founded in 1939 as part of the Ministry of Information whose aim was to make films of special interest for audiences in what was then the British Empire. Its films were distributed by the Colonial Office of Information. Film was to be in the 'front line' of war propaganda. In 1957 the director George Pearson commented that the establishment of the CFU:

> was tangible recognition of the potential power of the screen, in mass persuasion equal, if not greater than the orator, in propaganda second only to the Press, and in clarity of instruction abler than the verbal lecture ... The films were shown to native audiences by travelling cinema vans that penetrated deep into the African interior, far from the populated coast towns.[12]

The function of the CFU's films was essentially that of education and propaganda. Between its birth in 1939 and closure in 1955, the CFU produced a total of 280 short films, and eighty-five of these were war related. The original purpose of the CFU was to explain the war to audiences in the colonies, to tell them why Britain was fighting and invite their support.

The CFU produced and distributed a number of goodwill films in which they tried to convince colonial African audiences that they were involved in the war. The CFU requested the production of films that showed how Africans were integrating into the British way of life. For example, in 1941 George Pearson directed *An African in London* which showed a West African, portrayed by the Guyanese actor Robert Adams, being given a short tour of London landmarks. The purpose of the film was to show African audiences that everyone was a member of the British Empire and 'that all may look to the imperial centre, that all are welcome there, and that there is opportunity for all irrespective of race or creed'.[13] *West African Editors* (1944) showed a group of West African journalists, including Nnamdi Azikiwe, editor of the journal *West African Pilot*, on a visit to Britain. Another theme from the CFU was gratitude for the support the colonies in West Africa were giving to the war effort. *Katsina Tank* (1943), featuring the London-based Nigerian air-raid warden E.I. Ekpenyon (see Chapter 6), showed how gifts from the colonies were being used in Britain.

From 1943 to 1945, a monthly 16mm silent newsreel called *The British Empire at War*, designed for showing in mobile cinema vans, was added to the CFU's repertoire. It ran to twenty-five editions and included two directed by George Pearson in 1943: *Nurse Ademola* and *Pilot Officer Peter Thomas*. Both films are now thought to be lost. Further investigation reveals that the nurse in *Nurse Ademola* was actually an African princess, Omo-Oba Adenrele Ademola, daughter of the Alake of Abeokuta, the paramount chief of northern Nigeria. In 1938 it was reported in *The British Journal of Nursing* that the chief, 'who is interested in hospital services and hygiene', decided that his daughter should train as a nurse in Guy's Hospital in London. Several photographs of Nurse Ademola are held in the Imperial War Museum's photograph collection.[14]

Another African pioneer was the subject of *Pilot Officer Peter Thomas*. This featured Leading Aircraftman Adeniyi Peter Thomas, who was the first commissioned Nigerian in the Royal Air Force. Originally a civil servant in Lagos, he was given permission to sit the RAF entrance exam and passed. In November 1941 he was photographed, for the purpose of propaganda, making a radio broadcast and was described as 'part of the RAF Volunteer Reserve'. In February 1945 the League of Coloured Peoples reported in their *News Letter* that 'Flying Officer Peter Thomas, of West Africa' had 'died as a result of a flying accident' in training in south-west England.[15]

The West Indies were not forgotten. Learie Constantine was the subject of the CFU's *Learie Constantine* (1944), also directed by George Pearson, for distribution in the West Indies. The film is silent and it would have been shown to audiences throughout Britain's Caribbean colonies, often in venues without sound equipment. The MOI was quick to realise that there was great propaganda value in the fact that Constantine, known as a famous cricketer, was deeply involved in a vital wartime task – helping to integrate West Indians into British society and the workforce. *Learie Constantine* shows the day-to-day work of Constantine: meeting factory workers, listening to their problems and taking part in a charity cricket match.

Most of the CFU's wartime output has been lost, but thanks to the National Film and Television Archive (NFTVA), prints of *Learie Constantine* and *Springtime in an English Village* (1944) have survived. Viewing copies have recently been made available in the BFI Mediatheque's *Black Britain* collection and on the internet. *Springtime in an English Village* is a remarkable film for its depiction of a black girl taking part in an age-old rural tradition. In the spring of 1944 the CFU made this propaganda short in the tiny village of Stanion in Northamptonshire, and their footage, unseen for many years and restored by the NFTVA, shows the coronation of Britain's first black Queen of the May. The child has been identified as Stephanie Antia, the Liverpool-born 8-year-old daughter of Stephan Antia, who was an African merchant seaman, and his English wife Mary. Stephanie and her twin sister Constance, who is also featured in the film, had been evacuated to Stanion in 1940. Though the village children had never seen a black person before, they accepted the twins and chose Stephanie as May Queen in 1944. After Stephanie had been discovered living in America in 2009, the following interview with Catherine Collins appeared in the *Northants Evening Telegraph*:

> They attended lessons at St Peter's Church in the village and Stephanie made national headlines when she was crowned May Queen in 1944. The event was also captured on film – called *Springtime in an English Village* – which was made for people living in the British colonies and which has recently been digitally restored by the British Film Institute. Stephanie, who now lives in Maryland, America, with her family, said: 'I had a very interesting and happy childhood and teenage years. I don't feel being evacuated affected my childhood years, especially being with such wonderful people like the Keebles who had such love for me and wanted to adopt me. Of course I missed my parents – what child doesn't? – even though they used to visit whenever possible. Being a twin we were separated and lived opposite each other with different families, but we still played and did things together.'[16]

CHAPTER 11

FOR THE MOTHER COUNTRY:
THE HOME FRONT IN WEST AFRICAN AND CARIBBEAN COLONIES

During the 1920s and throughout most of the 1930s the colonies in West Africa and the Caribbean barely featured on the agenda of policy makers in Whitehall and Westminster. For example, when the Caribbean or British West Indies, as it was then known, was considered, it was usually for the state of plantation agriculture and labour problems. In short, the colonies were seen as an unchanging part of the British Empire with no voice of their own in a rapidly changing world.

The Great Depression of the 1930s was a period of crisis everywhere, but it hit the British West Indies very hard. The islands were largely run by and for plantation-owning, white, upper-class Englishmen and they relied on a black labour force that had no voting rights. In order to vote citizens had to own property or earn a monthly salary greater than $150. Trade unions were outlawed. Black workers were terribly exploited and forced to live in conditions similar to those that existed during the era of plantation slavery. The hardships led to revolt and rebellion – also known as the 'hurricane of protest' – in Guyana, Trinidad, St Kitts, Jamaica, St Vincent and Barbados. There had been a long history of resistance to injustice in Britain's colonies and the 1930s witnessed a dramatic rise in organised labour militancy with the increasingly influential and militant trade unions demanding industrial rights, decent pay, improvements in working conditions and social justice. In the late 1930s the British West Indies witnessed riots and social unrest. Consequently, a Royal Commission of Inquiry, headed by Lord Moyne, was called to examine regional social and economic conditions. Early in 1939 the British government acknowledged Lord Moyne's recommendations for reform in the British West Indies. In spite of the poverty and exploitation they experienced, many people growing up there and in other parts of the empire were, said Randolph Beresford from Guyana, 'more British than the British. As a boy, we celebrated Queen Victoria's birthday. We were told we were a part of Britain, we were British.'[1]

In 1939 many in Britain still viewed the West Indies and other colonies as backwaters of the British Empire, but when war was declared on Germany, in spite of unrest, the people of the empire immediately rallied behind the 'mother country'. All citizens in the colonies made important contributions, but this has been mostly overlooked and neglected by historians.[2]

Many black people from across the empire supported the British war effort because they saw the possibility of post-war reform and independence for their homelands. Others were motivated by a sense of duty to overcome the struggle between the so-called 'free world' and fascism. The people of the empire strongly identified with the mother country and wanted to protect their homelands from Nazi occupation.

Connie Mark was born in Kingston, Jamaica, and was 19 years old when she joined the British army there in 1943.[3] She said: 'we were brought up that England was our Mother Country and obviously when your mother has problems, you've got to come and help her.'[4] Another Jamaican, Sam King, was also keen to support the British: 'I don't think the British Empire was perfect, but it was better than Nazi Germany. So I wanted to join the armed service. But you could not because you were from the colony. So I had to do farming.'[5]

However, Austin Clarke has given a more cynical account of how some West Indian islanders felt. Describing the sudden changes in life on the island of Barbados, which was also known as 'Little England', he says:

> All of a sudden we had an army. The police were put on alert. Sea scouts became self-important, as they were taken deeper out into the harbour and told a few things about spotting enemy ships by the harbour police. And we heard that our leader, Grantley Adams, sent a cable up to the King, and told the King, 'Go on, England, Little England is behind you.' We were English. The allegiance and the patriotism that our leader, Mr Grantley Adams, had imprisoned us with had been cabled to the Colonial Office in London. We were the English of Little England. Little black Englishmen.[6]

From the start, people in the British West Indies supported the war effort and, like Sam King, they helped by farming or through fund-raising or sending food parcels. From the islands came sugar, cotton, oil and bauxite (aluminium ore). Eventually, when Britain realised they couldn't beat Nazi

Germany without help, they appealed for recruits from the colonies. These recruits made the long and difficult journey to Britain as volunteers in order to perform military or civilian roles. From the Caribbean, around 10,000 men and women joined the armed services while thousands more served as merchant seamen. Around 2,500 came to work in factories in England or as foresters in Scotland.[7]

At first the war may have seemed a long way away to the people of African and West Indian colonies, but wartime restrictions and German U-boats patrolling the Atlantic and Caribbean islands brought the war to the remotest parts of the British Empire. Trinidad was considered one of the most vulnerable islands in the West Indies because it was a major source of oil and was a supply base for the British. Also in Trinidad, Calypsonians mocked Hitler and Nazi Germany with their songs, including Lord Ziegfeld's *Hitler – Calypso* (1939) ('You're only staying in Germany/Demanding everybody's colony/But do, boy, don't tackle over here/For you wouldn't meet it like Czechoslovakia') and Lord Beginner's *Run Your Run Hitler – Calypso* (1940) ('That man Hitler, who known as the Great Dictator/And the German nation he have in real confusion/He know that he cannot win, why don't he beg Mister Chamberlain?/Surety with diplomacy, we will capture Germany').[8]

The true nature of war really hit home to Connie Mark when her best friend was killed:

> The first time the reality of war came to me was when I read in our local paper, *The Gleaner*, that Enid Edwards, from Port Antonio, died in a ship returning to Jamaica. The ship was torpedoed by the Germans. She was my best friend and we went to the same piano teacher. Enid studied at the Royal College of Music in London and passed all her exams with distinction. We were so proud of her and looked forward so much to her return to Jamaica. I cried for weeks.[9]

People living in the Caribbean islands, such as Barbados, Jamaica, Montserrat, Grenada and Trinidad, experienced a war not dissimilar to that of the mother country. They shared some of the conditions of life on the home front in Britain. Home Guards units were organised and air-raid drills and blackout routines were carried out. There were fears that the Germans might attack so they had air-raid sirens to warn people of these and introduced blackout regulations, air-raid precautions and employed air-raid wardens to enforce the rules. The wardens often visited towns and villages on the islands to see if anyone was breaking the rules by showing any light that might attract possible bombers. However, when the Guyanese actor Norman Beaton recalled the war in his autobiography, he described his father's role as an air-raid warden 'a totally useless exercise. Not one single plane ever came near Georgetown, and when it was rumoured that a torpedo had been discovered on the beach, the whole of Georgetown rushed down to the sea wall to have a look at the devilish engine.'[10]

Food and water rationing was also introduced. In addition to newspapers providing readers in the colonies with information, local government information departments also published and distributed news sheets, and these were especially important in the smaller islands of the Caribbean, which lacked a newspaper of their own. Propaganda in the form of poster campaigns and films produced by the Colonial Film Unit played an important role in gaining support and recruiting civilians across the empire for the war effort. In Jamaica there was an internment camp for German and Italian prisoners of war. German U-boats patrolling the Caribbean islands attacked passenger ships and destroyed shipping. Vital freight was destroyed, contributing to the shortages of basic commodities. An increase in the production of oil and bauxite in the West Indies drew German U-boats into American shipping lanes. In 1942 a Canadian ship called the *Cornwallis* was docked in Barbados harbour when a German U-boat hit it and sank it with torpedoes. The explosion could be heard right across Barbados and the islanders prepared for a German invasion. Austin Clarke has described the panic that followed:

All of a sudden people were running for their lives. They were in cars, on bicycles, and some were in donkey carts. The Germans had invaded Barbados ... We had been content to read about the war in the *Advocate*, in the photographs in the few copies of *Life* magazine that trickled into the island, in *Movietone* newsreels at the Empire Theatre, and every night on the BBC. This afternoon the people were running for the hills ... The Germans were coming, the men said ... and the island would be put in a concentration camp. We had heard about concentration camps on the BBC. And as in all other ways of life in the island, [those] who got to the hills first were the rich people. During the war, the rich people were the white people. After the war the black people laughed at the white people for getting to the hills first. They were 'blasted cowards,' the Black people said. 'More blasted coward than we poor people!'

Just a few hours later it became apparent that the Germans were not going to land in Barbados after all. 'They had just stopped by to torpedo a ship,' says Austin Clarke.[11]

In spite of being a small and impoverished part of the British Empire, the people and governments of the British West Indies offered substantial assistance to the British war effort. Some of this was reported in the wartime newsletters of the League of Coloured Peoples. As early as September

1940 Dr Harold Moody reported that in the British Colonial Empire of '60,000,000 souls', 44 million were to be found in Africa and the West Indies:

> [They] have subscribed over nine million pounds sterling, besides much goods, to Britain's war effort. Of this vast amount nearly one million pounds sterling, in addition to valuable produce and hospital supplies, have come from the impoverished people of the West Indies. It must be recognised that our people have made these incredible sacrifices, not only because of their love for Britain, but even more because they know something of what slavery means, and as human beings they are lovers of liberty.[12]

Two months later, the *News Letter* reported that over 100 large cases of clothing and blankets received from voluntary organisations in the West Indies had been distributed by the West India Committee among the bombed-out homeless of London: 'The West Indies and British Guiana have sent well over £150,000 for bombers and fighters, and over £96,000 for the Lord Mayor's Red Cross Fund, and have made gifts and loans, free of interest, to the Home Government, totalling £1,228,000.' The same newsletter added that the BBC had announced – on 29 October – that Jamaica (which had already provided eight planes) 'is now aiming at the provision of a whole squadron'.[13]

Interviews

The following interviews with Loleta Jemmott (Barbados), Olu Richards (Sierra Leone), Randoll Dacosta (Barbados), Cerene Palmer (Jamaica) and Brenda Clough (Guyana) were conducted in the London borough of Southwark and extracts from some of them were included in the Cuming Museum's 2008 exhibition 'Keep Smiling Through – Black Londoners on the Home Front 1939–1945'. The main purpose of the interviews was to explore some of the ways in which the Second World War impacted on the people of the West Indian and West African colonies. The similarities with people in the British Isles are the most striking features of the interviews – the threat of a German invasion, food rationing, air-raid blackouts and warnings, the hatred of Adolf Hitler – and yet the lives and experiences of British citizens throughout the empire at this time have been excluded from books about the Second World War, and there has been no acknowledgement of the major contribution these West Indian and West African people made to the British war effort.

Loleta Jemmott (Barbados)

Loleta Jemmott was born in the parish of St Michael, 1 mile from Bridgetown, the capital of Barbados. She was 6 years old when the war started: 'I can remember the church bells ringing out and people crying out and that was the announcement that the war had started.' Loleta says that, during the war, parents and grandparents didn't speak openly to children: 'They didn't let us hear what was going on. Now we would like to ask, but our parents and grandparents have died. There it is.' She remembers the blackout: 'We had lamps, no electricity, and you had to keep the lamp low and dim and we always tried to speak in lower tones in case the Germans landed [laughs]. There was a fear of the German Boats in the water around Barbados and we lived close to the beach.' In 1942 a Canadian ship sailing near Barbados harbour was torpedoed and sunk by a German U-boat. It was a major incident that made news across the Caribbean. Loleta remembers:

> We didn't have any air raids, but the sinking of the Cornwallis near the harbour was the first real incident we had. It was about six o'clock in the evening and I can remember hearing this loud bang and vibration, a blast. We thought maybe the soldiers are practicing. As we lived so near, from the beach, within minutes we heard that the Germans are here, they've bombed a boat. It was very disturbing. Families were advised to stay in their homes until it was safe.

Loleta remembers food rationing: 'We had coupons in alphabetical order so on the day your surname came up you went to places like doctors surgeries and schools to queue up to get your coupons and that would have given you rations for rice, sugar and things like that. Kerosene was rationed. Rice. Clothing. Your parents would try and be early into the queue.' BBC radio programmes, relayed by cable into Barbadian homes, kept families in touch with the rest of the world:

> Whether you were poor or not, Rediffusion brought us instant news about the war from the BBC's Empire Service in England. We listened to concerts and classical music and on Sundays we could hear a half-hour service from St Martin-in-the-Fields, the church in Trafalgar Square, and we would dream about visiting London one day and going to St Martin-in-the-Fields.

Loleta was familiar with the term 'mother country': 'Yes, the term Mother Country was used because we were part of the British Empire. England was the land of milk and honey and we said it was the Mother Country.'

In 1956 Loleta travelled to London to train as a nurse. Loleta Jemmott was interviewed by Stephen Bourne on 20 February 2008.

Olu Richards (Sierra Leone)

Britain's colonies in West Africa – Gambia, Sierra Leone, the Gold Coast (now Ghana) and Nigeria – all supported the war effort, and served as staging posts and military bases. Olu Richards was born in Freetown, the capital city of Sierra Leone, and a major port on the Atlantic Ocean in West Africa. He was the son of a mechanical engineer. Olu was 5 years old in 1939 when the Second World War started: 'Sierra Leone was fully involved in the war and lots of soldiers were recruited from Sierra Leone. It was a strategic country. I was told that King George VI visited Freetown on at least one occasion during the war.' Olu remembers air-raid blackouts:

> You were not supposed to put your lights on in your houses. Most of these houses were timber and if the security men pass by in the evening and see a light they would come and knock on your door. 'Put out that light! Put out that light!' And most people during the blackout when they did not want people to know they had light they used candles or oil lamps but security sometimes spy in your house and see the light and come and knock on your door. There was no punishment.

Olu recalls the many security alerts, 'and when they suspect there was going to be some bombing or something bad they give a siren sound all over the country, especially in Freetown, and people should run indoors. If you are out in the street you should make sure that you put yourself in the gutter somewhere where you will not be seen standing up.'

At the Christian missionary school Olu attended they had air-raid drills:

> They told us what to do if you heard the siren or planes flying overhead. It was definitely frightening for a young child. Once or twice I had to lay flat in the gutter when I heard the aeroplane flying above. People panicked when they heard the aeroplanes flying above. They told everybody to have sandbags in their houses and if something suspicious dropped in their house you can just go and put sand over it.

Olu had an English education at his school:

We were taught in English and the literature was in English. We did British history as well. We had a book called 'The March of History' which started in Medieval times, to all the kings and queens of England right up to Victoria and King George VI. We were mostly taught by local African people but the Department of Education was run by Europeans.

Olu remembers a gun at the east end of Freetown:

It's still there, I think, as a monument, because they call the place Upgun. And there was another gun down at Kingtown which was pointing towards the Atlantic. So we were ready if there was any German planes coming to attack. Local men were trained to man the guns. This was colonial days and the British were in charge of everything and trained the men.

Rediffusion provided families with news of the war: 'We didn't have a wireless radio, we had Rediffusion. It was wired to the broadcasting station in Freetown, just like electricity wire, standing on poles, and most houses had this. It was a box with one station, the BBC's West Africa service. Mainly news and some music.'

Olu recalls that Adolf Hitler was viewed as 'a wicked person' who 'brought disaster to the world'. He says that after the American athlete Jesse Owens did well at the Olympics in 1936, word got back to the people of Freetown that Hitler did not like Owens' success because he was a black man: 'The news got back to us that Hitler would use the skin of a black man to make shoes. People took it very seriously. He was an evil man. They used to nickname a bad person "Hitler" or "You're wicked like Hitler" [laughs].'

When Olu came to London in 1958 he could see many bomb sites, especially in the East End. He said he saw the results of war. Independence came to Sierra Leone in 1964. Regarding the term 'mother country', Olu explains:

Freed slaves were taken to Freetown and although they were in Freetown they regarded England as their Mother Country. They were British subjects and so some said they were going back to their Mother Country. So those liberated Africans who were taken to Freetown in the beginning regarded England as their Mother Country. The term was still being used when I was growing up.

Olu Richards was interviewed by Stephen Bourne on 19 February 2008.

Randoll Dacosta (Barbados)

Randoll Dacosta was born in Store Gap, near Portadown Hill in Barbados: 'My father was what we call a hawker. A person that has a donkey cart and he would go to the farm and buy yams and potatoes and things like that and then he'd go round the village and sell them.' Randoll was 3 years old when the war started:

> My parents talked about the war, but not to us, but we would listen in at the door. There was no electricity in the streets. We had lamps and we used kerosene oil to light it. We didn't have blackout curtains. My mother used meal bags, flour bags, bleach them out and sew them together to block out the windows. Radios was very scarce. Only a few people could afford them. My brother in law used to work in the wharfside, in the harbour, and so anything that goes on in the town, he would tell us. That's how we heard about the war.

Randoll has vivid memories of the German U-boat sinking the Canadian ship *Cornwallis* in 1942:

> The Cornwallis would bring provisions to Barbados, like bully beef, cod fish, biscuits. And they bomb it in the harbour. Bridgetown harbour. We lived on a hill so you can see the whole of Bridgetown. So you hear this big bang and see black smoke and everybody wondered what was going on. One of my neighbours she came home from work and everybody wanted to know what was going on. Then we heard it was the Cornwallis. They torpedoed it right in the harbour. I didn't see the ship myself but people used to go down to the seaside to get the bully beef that wash into shore and carry it home because people wanted provisions. Food was short.

Randoll says that the sinking of the *Cornwallis* caused some conflict between the British and the Americans: 'The Americans didn't think the British were looking after Barbados as they should. So they wanted to come in and secure Barbados more. The Americans had their own submarines in the harbour, but then the British said this was our island, we don't want you to invade it, so that caused an upset between the British and the Americans.'

At the end of the war Barbados celebrated and Randoll remembers school ending earlier than usual: 'People beat drums and let off fireworks. So we knew that the war was finished. I remember a kind of enjoyment.' Randoll was 15 when he left Barbados to join his sister in London: 'My first impression was seeing all these factories but I never knew they were the chimneys of the houses. I saw bomb sites all over the place.' He says that when he was a child England was referred to as the mother country:

> To my understanding they said the Queen was the mother to all of the West Indies, so I think that's where the term come from. That the Queen is your mother. Because everywhere you go in Barbados there is a photograph of the Queen. But I think Mother Country came from Queen Victoria, because Barbados was known as Little England. Because everything we were taught at school was English. My best friend in Barbados was white. We were at school together, we eat together, we play together. So I didn't know anything about difference or prejudice until I come to England. I wasn't taught that.

Randoll Dacosta was interviewed by Stephen Bourne on 6 March 2008.

Cerene Palmer (Jamaica)

Cerene Palmer was born in Whitby District, Manchester, Jamaica. Two of Cerene's uncles, Clinton Ken Enright (her mother's brother) and Joe Palmer (her father's brother), joined the Royal Air Force: 'I remember going to the post box to look for letters from Uncle Ken who was in the Royal Air Force, but when he came home on leave he didn't speak about it. I think he had a rough time. He might have been homesick. Many things for black ones were difficult.'

Cerene's grandmother, Tammar Palmer, was born in the Victorian era and died at the age of 89 in the 1970s:

> My grandmother used to say, 'I'm going to England', and we say 'but you don't know anybody there!' [laughs]. She said she don't mind because she is British and England is the Mother Country. The term Mother Country was while slavery was abolished and we became a single British colony, in the British West Indies, and we'd say 'England is our Mother Country'. It could have come from Queen Victoria because my grandmother used to refer to her a lot. She was so proud of 'Mrs Queen Victoria'. She used to curtsey every time she referred to 'Mrs Queen Victoria'. During the war she would have been in her sixties so she must have been born when Queen Victoria ruled.

Cerene remembers that evacuees from Kingston were sent to the rural parts of Jamaica because of the fear of a German invasion. She also remembers rationing:

We had food shortages during the war and one of the things that I remember is sugar. The native people make their own sugar. We'd squeeze the sugar cane to make the juice to get sugar. We know how to make sugar. You have people coming round buying sugar, but somehow it went. It dried up. We couldn't get any sugar anymore and then we had these people come with granulated, white sugar. We had flour. Saltfish. And because we were country people we had our own produce. We had our own oranges, avocado pears, bread fruit, banana, tangerine, mandarin, satsuma. Anything you can think of, we had. We cultivate our own plot of land. My grandfather was a farmer, and his father before him but, by the time my father and mother come along, they were looking for something better to do. That's why they migrate from the country to the town area. To make a better life.

Cerene heard about the German boats and submarines in the sea:

but in those days when adults speak, children were not allowed to listen. And when we hear those things they said 'Go away'. And some they say no, we have to know because when the plane is bombing, we call them rogue planes, we have to know to run and hide. But we didn't get any rogue planes. We used to hear about U boat but we didn't think about it because we didn't know what it means. Children were definitely protected from the war.

Cerene remembers the British commissioner coming to the school building and inviting the whole village, or two or three villages, to come and listen:

the speaker tell us how bad the war was, and what they needed, and what cooperation they needed from us because we used to send oranges and fruits and things. I remember my godmother picking the best oranges for King George and 'Lady Queen Elizabeth'. We used to laugh at that. They needed iron and West Indians used a lot of iron parts. So whoever had iron parts, a spoon, whatever, they sent it. In the town area they probably gave money and knitted socks and balaclavas [for the war effort] but in the country area we gave the food we produced. We were helping the Mother Country because we were already under that umbrella and one day you might want to come to the Mother Country. We didn't want the Germans to invade England like they did France. Although we sometimes didn't understand what was going on, they would throw invasion in because my grandmother always say 'If a bad man call you, run!' [laughs] If you see anybody you don't know, don't speak to them, because you don't know where they're coming from.

At that time in Jamaica there were many nationalities; Cerene remembers Germans, Irish, English, Greek, Chinese and Japanese, 'a whole lot of them. They all pulled together for the war effort. Every last person.' News about the war came from the radio and the theatre:

> Every West Indian loved the theatre. Anything to do with art. Acting. Painting. Not every house might have a radio but everyone's ears were pealed to it. At the theatre we called it the intermission. The intermission would come on and before the film started, the war newsreels would come up on the screen and you'd hear the voice telling you and that's when we know what ships look like, and we see the bombing and people running. The newsreels came on again after the film, before you go out. We were really kept informed.

Hitler and Mussolini were hated:

> You don't want to know what we thought of Hitler [laughs]. You'd hear men say 'You just bring him to me [laughs] and I'll chop him right down the middle!' There was a song in Jamaica, I think it was a calypso, 'Mussolini/You know you're wrong/Mussolini/Don't be so strong'. Really nice lyrics it have to it. All of a sudden they'd put it on and let it blast.

When Jamaicans heard that the war was finished and Hitler was dead, everybody wanted to know how he died:

> because everybody wanted a piece of him to make sure he died [laughs]. They wanted to make sure it was him. They hung Mussolini so everybody could see him. You knew he was dead. When I came here [to England] as a young woman, I heard that Hitler had not died. Then another story was that he died and dogs ate his body. So many versions of that story went around because they said his body was burnt, but we couldn't be certain.

Cerene remembers a street celebration at the end of the war: 'We waved a branch of a tree and listened to calypsos. The whole island took part. When you find out that all that is not over your head anymore, then you go out and celebrate and, boy, the black person certainly know how to celebrate! [laughs].'

In 1964 Cerene travelled to London to train as a nurse. Cerene Palmer was interviewed by Stephen Bourne on 10 July 2008.

Brenda Clough (Guyana)

Brenda Clough was born in Georgetown, Guyana (formerly British Guiana): 'My parents didn't discuss the war with the children, it's just in the latter years that we asked a few questions – it was not a subject that was discussed very much.' Brenda's father worked as an engineer and because Guyana was a British colony everybody wanted to contribute to the war:

> Dad told us that he wanted to be part of the war effort, to be a soldier and fight abroad but he had recently been married and the people at the office where he went to 'sign up' didn't think it would be a good idea for a recently married young man to be going off to war. On that basis he wasn't able to be in the 'fighting' part of the war so the next thing he was able to do was to be a driver at the American base which was quite far up in the countryside towards the jungle area or 'the interior' as it's known; that was his contribution to the war which he enjoyed tremendously.
>
> Dad's uncle worked as a ship's pilot which involved taking out a smaller vessel to the larger vessels to unload their cargo as the sea level was too low to allow the larger vessels into the docks. One night Dad's uncle's ship was torpedoed by the enemy and he was killed. They had blackouts in the harbour as that was the only access there was, there was no landing strip in Georgetown so everything came in by boat to the country at that time. People relied on the ships for food they couldn't grow themselves and also for material to make clothing and for 'ready-made' garments; as these items became scarce people had to 'make do' so there was always a seamstress willing to make up an outfit for you. As a part of our staple diet, fish became quite scarce because the fishermen were unable to go out very far from shore to fish.

At school Brenda was taught from the *West Indian Reader*:

> We were taught the three Rs and we began our school day with assembly which consisted of singing hymns and *The Lord's Prayer*. Our education was based on the English curriculum so we learnt a lot about the English way of life. I remember reading a poem about a robin, which fascinated me, and then I experienced it by coming to England and seeing a real robin.

Brenda said there were well-educated people in Guyana who did not accept everything that existed in the country and tried to bring about independence:

> We were a British 'colony', just like some of the West Indian islands, so when we came to England as migrants there was good comradeship between us

even though we were thousands of miles from the West Indies. The common denominator we share is that we are all descended from slaves or slave owners. Geographically we are not West Indians but culturally we have many similarities. When we came to England in 1959 we settled in well at school and did not feel threatened in any way as there was no racial tension in Thornton Heath at that time, unlike in Notting Hill previously, possibly due to the fact that there were no black children in my school and very few black residents in the area. We came from a church-oriented background and worshipped as a family in a truly genuine Christian (all-white then) assembly at which my mother and father remained members until their deaths, approximately forty years. When we arrived in London we expected to see affluence in abundance but instead we were surprised to see war-damaged and derelict buildings, quite a different scenario from that widely believed at that time.

Brenda Clough was interviewed by Stephen Bourne on 5 March 2008.

IF HITLER HAD INVADED BRITAIN

Holocaust Memorial Day, held every February, was mainly set up to remember the 6 million Jewish men, women and children murdered by Hitler's Nazi regime and, while a great deal of information has been documented about Jewish victims, the Nazi's persecution and murder of other groups is still to be fully researched and documented. It has been estimated that at least another 5 million 'others' could have perished in Nazi concentration camps and these would have included communists, lesbians, gays, Jehovah's Witnesses, gypsies and people with physical or mental disabilities. According to the United States Holocaust Memorial Museum in Washington DC: 'The fate of black people from 1933 to 1945 in Nazi Germany and in German-occupied territories ranged from isolation to persecution, sterilization, medical experimentation, incarceration, brutality and murder. However, there was no systematic program for their elimination as there was for Jews and other groups.'[1]

When Hitler was the ruler of Germany (1933–45), many black and mixed-race Germans were rounded up by the Gestapo (the German secret police) and forcibly sterilised. In 1937 local authorities in Germany were asked to submit lists of all children of African descent. These children were taken from their homes or schools without the consent of their parents and, if the child was identified as of African descent, they were taken to a hospital and sterilised. At least 400 mixed-race children were forcibly sterilised in the Rhineland area alone by the end of 1937, while 400 others 'disappeared', probably into Hitler's concentration camps.

Working as Extras in Nazi Propaganda Films

Some black Germans found that they could avoid internment in concentration camps by working as extras in Nazi propaganda films. Two mixed-race German sisters, Doris Reiprich and Erika Ngambi ul Kuo, have provided first-hand accounts of what it was like to be black and living in Nazi Germany. Their father, a Cameroonian, had settled in Hamburg in 1891 and married their mother, a white East Prussian, in 1914. When Hitler came to power in 1933, Doris says hardly any Africans, including her father, returned to Africa. 'What were they to do there?' she asks. 'Who would have paid for their trips? So they struggled along in films or the circus.' Between 1933 and 1945, *Staatsauftragsfilme* produced nearly 100 films by order of the Propaganda Ministry. Many films set in colonial Africa went into production and Doris believes that the demand for African extras and their mixed-race children helped most of them avoid internment in Nazi death camps.

Others were not so fortunate. Doris and Erika's mixed-race friend and her husband, a Dutchman, were 'picked up'. Doris says the Nazis accused them of all sorts of things and called their friend a 'nigger whore'. The couple were arrested and interned in a concentration camp. At the other extreme, Doris remembers the fun they had during the making of the propaganda films: 'On our breaks the Africans would get their drums and we'd sing in front of the studios. People would come running from all the productions. They loved to listen. We earned good money, had fun.' She adds: 'One time about two hundred and fifty black prisoners of war from the United States were brought in because they needed film extras. Those poor fellows were glad to be with us, since they got to eat and play football. We also put money together to buy things for them.' Fortunately, as well as managing to avoid internment, Doris avoided sterilisation, and had two children. Her pride at becoming a mother says it all: 'My daughter has blonde hair and blue eyes. I would love to have shown her to Hitler and told him, "Here's a German girl, but she's not for you!"'[2]

Theodor Michael

Theodor Michael was born in Germany in 1925 and also survived the war by working in the film industry. During the Nazi era Theodor appeared in dozens of German films. It was to be the start of a career as one of Germany's most durable character actors. By the age of 10 Theodor was an orphan. To avoid the dangers of living in Nazi Germany, his brother James and two sisters joined circuses and left the country. It took 15 years for Theodor to be reunited with them. Theodor had to survive alone in Nazi Germany and found a safety net by becoming a film extra. In 1943 many African and black American prisoners of war were employed as extras in the German film classic *Munchhausen*, directed by Josef von Baky. Theodor is visible as an exotic slave boy in this ambitious colour production. The making of this film had been ordered by Joseph Goebbels, Hitler's Minister of Propaganda and Public Enlightenment, to celebrate the twenty-fifth anniversary of UFA, the prestigious German production company. It was the most spectacular of the films made during the Nazi regime. After the closure of all the film studios Theodor was sent to work in a munitions factory. As a non-Aryan he risked being arrested by the Gestapo. He recalled in the 1997 documentary film *Hitler's Forgotten Victims*, directed by David Okuefuna:

> You just lived one day to the other and you were happy if you were still alive. I was liberated by Russians and they were surprised to see a black man still alive. It was very hard to convince them that I hadn't done anything special to be still alive and, after the war, people confronted me with war crimes done by Germans, my nation. I was a victim but they happened in my name.

In *Hitler's Forgotten Victims* Theodor described himself as one of the oldest working actors in Germany, having just acted in a German stage production of *Driving Miss Daisy*.

John Welch

A story that has remained untold is that of John Welch, who was born in New York in 1906. He was the younger brother of the New York-born singer Elisabeth Welch (see Chapter 8) who made London her home in 1933. Elisabeth's success in Britain enabled her to help finance her brother's music tuition in Berlin – where he had travelled in 1932 to study piano. That same year Elisabeth visited John and enjoyed some success with a cabaret engagement there. Elisabeth received rave reviews but, following the rise of Hitler and the Nazis, it became impossible for a black entertainer to make an appearance in Germany. Meanwhile, John Welch remained in Germany for twelve years and, at first, went about his business as a music student and then as a pianist without any trouble. Just before he was arrested by the Nazis shortly after the outbreak of the Second World War, he had nothing but praise for Germany:

> Before Hitler came into power, the Negro was treated exceptionally well. But even today, just as in any other European country … the Negro may have

a room in any of the best hotels; he may attend the theatre and be seated in any part of the house; he may go into any bar or visit any restaurant, café or night club and be waited on courteously and attend schools and universities. In short, he may do anything he is big enough to do as long as he carries himself respectably and has the money and means to do it with.

It is likely that Welch was 'shielded' in 1930s Germany by his American status, but soon after he wrote the above he was arrested by the Nazis, accused of being an enemy agent and sent to a concentration camp. He spent several years in the camp, during which time his health suffered; the cold weather he was exposed to caused arthritis in his hands which ruined his ability to play the piano. In 1944 Welch survived his incarceration when he was repatriated to the United States with 661 American passengers who had been interned in France and Germany. The American government traded them for German prisoners of war. On board the Swedish ship SS *Gripsholm* that arrived in New York there were eleven other African American men and one black woman (Evelyn Anderson Hayman). John Welch died in 1999 at the age of 92.[3]

Paul Robeson in Nazi Germany

John Welch may have avoided being molested by the Nazis in the 1930s, but certain famous African American visitors to Germany discovered that their celebrity status did not protect them from hostility. Although Hitler spoke favourably of Paul Robeson in 1932, he was also reported as saying: 'Negroes must be definitely third-class people ... a hopeless lot. I don't hate them. I pity the poor devils.'[4] Two years later, a group of storm troopers showed hatred and contempt for Robeson when he was forced to spend a day in Berlin on his way to Moscow. In 1930, on his previous visit to Germany, the Nazis were in the minority and Hitler was regarded as a fanatic who was not taken seriously. A lot had happened in the four years he was away. In 1934 Robeson likened Berlin to America's Deep South. The storm troopers gathered menacingly on the station platform. Robeson and his friend Marie Seton were waiting for Robeson's wife Essie to join them. He said to Seton: 'This is like Mississippi. It's how a lynching begins. If either of us moves, or shows fear, they'll go further. We must keep our heads.'[5] Robeson and his companions made a fortunate escape when their train arrived, but he had been preparing for the worst and fully expected a violent confrontation with the storm troopers.

Paul Robeson and Hitler's Black Book

In September 1945 Hitler's 'blacklist', the *Sonderfahndungsliste* G.B. (literally translated as the Special Search List G.B.), was discovered. Known after the war as the *Black Book*, it had been compiled by the Gestapo and listed 2,820 British subjects and European exiles living in Britain who were to be automatically arrested following the completion of Operation Sealion, the German invasion of England. Winston Churchill was to be placed into the custody of Amt VI (Foreign Military Intelligence), but the vast majority of the people listed in the *Black Book* would be placed into the custody of Amt IV (Gestapo) and these included Paul Robeson. The *Black Book* listed such figures as Sigmund Freud (the Jewish founder of psychoanalysis), Vera Brittain (feminist writer and pacifist) and Bertrand Russell (philosopher, historian and pacifist). From the world of arts and literature, the book included Noel Coward, who opposed appeasement and was an armed forces entertainer, guilty also for his homosexuality and connections with MI5; E.M. Forster, the novelist who was also 'guilty' of homosexuality; and literary figures like H.G. Wells, Virginia Woolf, Aldous Huxley, Stephen Spender, Rebecca West and the left-wing actress Sybil Thorndike.[6]

If Hitler Had Invaded Britain

It is not known how many people of African descent in Germany and occupied Europe died at the hands of the Nazis during the Holocaust. No records exist. It has been estimated, however, that there were between 20,000 and 25,000 black people living in Germany when Hitler came to power: some were Africans who had travelled from the German colonies; others were French African troops who had settled in Germany after the First World War; some came from other parts of the world and were working or studying in Germany, often as entertainers and musicians. Many of them would have been persecuted, sterilised, brutalised and murdered during the Nazi regime.

For documenting the experiences of black Germans and revealing their fate in Nazi Germany, thanks must be given to David Okuefuna for his 1997 documentary film *Hitler's Forgotten Victims*, as well as three books: May Opitz, Katharina Oguntoye and Dagmar Schultz's *Showing Our Colours – Afro-German Women Speak Out* (1992); Hans J. Massaquoi's *Destined to Witness – Growing Up Black in Nazi Germany* (2001); and Clarence Lusane's *Hitler's Black Victims* (2002). However, historians of the Second World War have yet to investigate and explore what would have been the fate of Britain's black population if Hitler had invaded.

A German invasion of Britain came very close. After Germany had invaded and occupied France, it was only a matter of time before they crossed the English Channel. Hitler was confident that his plan to invade Britain in September 1940 would be successful and, chillingly, had made arrangements to uproot Nelson's column from Trafalgar Square and erect it in Berlin. In 1972 the historian Norman Longmate gave an absorbing and astonishing account of the effects of a German invasion on Britain in *If Britain Had Fallen*. However, it did not acknowledge the fate of Britain's black population. In a letter to the author in 2006 he explained:

> Yours is the first [letter] to ask what would have happened to black UK residents in the event of a successful German invasion. The answer is, I'm afraid, that I cannot be much help. In all the documents on German plans, which cover such matters as the Welsh language, I have not come across any which refer to the presence of people of different colour. I can find no reference to what was then called the colour problem in Martin Kitchen *Nazi Germany at War* (1995), but I think there is no doubt the Nazi 'master race' philosophy would have dismissed the black races as inferior, indeed they were visibly 'non-Aryan' and the one reference I have found brackets the negroes with the Jews. The Nazis complained about jazz as 'Negroid-Jewish jazz music' as corrupting (Kitchen, p.179). Hitler is known to have registered disgust when a black athlete [Jesse Owens] was successful in the 1936 Olympics. To sum up, I think the Nazis gave no particular attention to the black races simply because, unlike the Slavs or the Jews, they were barely visible in Europe. They would, in the event of occupying Britain, have, I think, been rounded up but as an afterthought after the Jews, with whom the Nazis were insanely obsessed, had been dealt with.[7]

In spite of the documentation that exists about what happened to black Germans under Nazi rule, and the inclusion of Paul Robeson in the *Black Book*, historians of the Second World War have consistently overlooked or avoided the fate of black British people if there had been a German occupation. However, black British citizens, including those in the former colonies, were fully aware of what their fate would have been if Hitler had invaded. It is because so little attention has been given to this subject that their fears have never been reported in the history books or in the media, except on one revealing occasion. In the television discussion programme *Here-Say*, shown on BBC2 in 1990, ex-servicemen and women from the former African and Caribbean colonies debated the pros and cons of supporting the British war effort with members of a younger, more critical (and cynical) generation. During the programme the British-born Lilian Bader (see Chapter 3), frustrated with the lack of understanding from some of the younger members of the audience, expressed in no uncertain terms why she had joined the WAAF: 'We [black people] would have ended up in the ovens.' It is the only occasion in British television history that this reality has been expressed.[8] If Hitler had invaded England black British citizens would have been vulnerable. If Paul Robeson was included in Hitler's *Black Book*, then it is likely that other prominent black people, such as Dr Harold Moody and Learie Constantine, would also have ended up in the hands of the Gestapo. The rest, including my Aunt Esther, would have been rounded up and interned in concentration camps or worse.

ENDNOTES

Introduction

1 Arthur Bourne quoted in Norman Longmate, *The Doodlebugs – The Story of the Flying-Bombs* (Hutchinson, 1981), p.250.

2 Angus Calder, *The People's War* (Jonathan Cape, 1969), p.205.

3 No official figure exists for the number of black people of African descent living in Britain in 1939. Unlike the United States, the ethnicity of British citizens has never been a requirement for a birth certificate, nor was it recorded in the early census returns. Historians do not agree on an accurate figure. In *Black Britannia* (1972) Edward Scobie estimates that in the years 1914 to 1945 there were 20,000 black people in Britain; in *Wartime Britain 1939–1945* (2004) Juliet Gardiner claims that at the outbreak of the Second World War there were no more than 8,000. Dr Hakim Adi, Reader in the History of Africa and the African Diaspora at Middlesex University and a founder member of the Black and Asian Studies Association, has suggested to the author that the most realistic estimate for 3 September 1939 is around 15,000, while Jeffrey Green, author of *Black Edwardians*, informs the author that, in his opinion, the figure is at least 40,000.

4 Source: *Map of Black Families in London* from a report entitled *Negro Families in Cardiff and London in 1935* by Nancie Hare quoted in Howard Bloch, 'Black People in Canning Town and Custom House between the Wars', *Association for the Study of African, Caribbean and Asian Culture and History in Britain*, Newsletter 14 (January 1996), p.5. Regrettably the report appears to have been lost. There is no copy in the British Library and the author's efforts to trace the copy seen by Howard Bloch in the Newham Local Studies Library have been unsuccessful.

5 Harold Macmillan memorandum, 14 September 1942, Public Record Office, CO 876/14.

6 'My Black Uncle', posted on the BBC website: *WW2 The People's War*.

Chapter I

1 Edward Scobie, *Black Britannia – A History of Blacks in Britain* (Johnson Publishing, 1972), p.148. See also Stephen Bourne, *Dr Harold Moody* (Southwark Council, 2008) and Sam Morris, 'Moody – The Forgotten Visionary', in *New Community*, Vol. 1, No 3 (Spring 1972), pp.193–196.

2 Jeffrey Green, interview with the author, 22 June 2008. Green is the author of *Black Edwardians – Black People in Britain 1901–1914* (Frank Cass, 1998).

3 David A. Vaughan, *Negro Victory – The Life Story of Dr Harold Moody* (Independent Press, 1950), p.33.

4 *Hidden History: Dr Harold Moody*, BBC Knowledge television documentary, 25 September 2000.

5 Dr Harold Moody, *100 Great Black Britons*, www.100greatblackbritons.com.

6 *The Keys* was the League of Coloured Peoples' journal from July 1933 to September 1939. Renamed the *News Letter* in October 1939, it was produced until 1950. These journals and the League's annual reports are the only surviving primary sources of information about the League. For a more detailed analysis of Dr Moody and the League, see Roderick J. Macdonald, 'Dr Harold Arundel Moody and the League of Coloured Peoples, 1931–47: A Retrospective View', in *Race and Class*, Vol. 14, No 3 (1973), pp.291–310, and Anne Spry Rush, 'Imperial Identity in Colonial Minds: Harold Moody and the League of Coloured Peoples, 1931–50', in *Twentieth Century British History*, Vol. 13, No 4 (2002), pp.356–383.

7 League of Coloured Peoples, *News Letter*, 23 (August 1941), pp.98–99.

8 Charles 'Joe' Moody, interviewed in *Lest We Forget*, a Channel 4 documentary about black participation in the Second World War, 8 November 1990.

9 Ibid.

10 Ibid.

11 Ibid.

12 Joe Moody served in the infantry and the artillery in England and Africa, then in Italy and finally in Egypt, where he became a major in 1945. At the end of the war he settled in Jamaica with B Company of the Caribbean Regiment. He became a colonel in 1961 and was awarded an OBE in 1966 as the first commanding officer of the Jamaican Territorial Army.

13 Dr Moody's letter, dated 14 May 1940, was reprinted in the *News Letter*, 9 (June 1940), p.39.

14 *News Letter*, 10 (July 1940), p.63.

15 *News Letter*, 14 (November 1940), p.25.

16 Vaughan, *Negro Victory*, p.117.

17 *News Letter*, 16 (January 1941), p.102.

18 'A Negro Recital', *The Times*, 7 March 1932, p.10.

19 *News Letter*, 25 (October 1941), p.3.

20 *News Letter*, 29 (February 1942), pp.98–99.

21 'Calling the West Indies', *News Letter*, 69 (June 1945), p.48.

22 *News Letter*, 21 (June 1941), p.56.

23 Vaughan, *Negro Victory*, p.55.

24 In addition to the English Heritage Blue Plaque and bronze portrait, Dr Moody is remembered in Peckham with a park and a street named in his honour. In addition to these tributes, on 31 October 2001 an Indian Bean Tree was planted in Chumleigh Gardens in Burgess Park, Southwark, in his memory. In 2007 Ronald Moody's 1946 bronze portrait of his brother was purchased by Southwark Council's Art Collection and displayed in the Dr Harold Moody section of the Cuming Museum's exhibition 'Keep Smiling Through – Black Londoners on the Home Front 1939–1945' (April–November 2008). In October 2009 the bronze portrait was given a permanent home in Peckham Library.

Chapter 2

1 Val Wilmer, 'Ivor Cummings', *The Independent*, 4 December 1992, p.31.
2 Mike Phillips and Trevor Phillips, *Windrush – The Irresistible Rise of Multi-Racial Britain* (HarperCollins, 1998), p.68.
3 Ibid., p.84.
4 Memo, Ivor Cummings (Assistant Welfare Officer) to J.L. Keith (Welfare Officer), 19 May 1941, PRO CO 859 76/6.
5 Phillips and Phillips, *Windrush*, p.84.
6 Rudolph Dunbar was born in British Guiana in 1907 and died in London in 1988.
7 Professor Ian Hall interviewed by Stephen Bourne, *Salutations*, BBC Radio 2, 2 October 1993.
8 Ibid.
9 For further information see Marika Sherwood, *Pastor Daniels Ekarte and the African Churches Mission* (The Savannah Press, 1994).
10 Charles Minto, born *c.* 1893 in Calabar, Nigeria, was a professional boxer and middleweight champion of Nigeria from 1915 to 1921. He settled in North Shields and in 1931 became the general secretary of the International Coloured Mutual Aid Association. He was later appointed as its president.
11 Rudolph Dunbar, 'Great Work By An African For The Up-Lift Of The People – New Institution For African Seamen In Britain', *The African Standard* (29 May 1942).
12 William 'Bill' Miller was born in East Street, Stonehouse, in Plymouth in 1890. His grandfather had been a slave who was granted his freedom at a church mission in Sierra Leone. His father, John Miller, born *c.* 1832, had found employment on a British ship on its way to England. In the 1891 census John, aged 59, gave his occupation as naval pensioner and chapel keeper. His wife, Sarah Ann, was from Yeovil in Somerset. In an interview with the author on 22 July 2002, Bill's son Claude said that he was told his African grandfather was a 'tall, slender man, well over six feet, and very religious. He died in 1914, one year before I was born.' During the First World War, Bill served in the Royal Flying Corps as an electrical fitter and rose to the rank of warrant officer. He died in 1970 at the age of 80.
13 Jonathan Wood, *Bill Miller – Black Labour Party Activist in Plymouth: A Biographical Sketch* (History and Social Action Publications for Labour Heritage, 2006), p.8.

14 Ibid.

15 Ibid., p.13.

16 Claude Miller, interview with Stephen Bourne, 22 July 2002.

17 Ernest Marke was born in Freetown, Sierra Leone, in 1902.

18 Val Wilmer, 'Ernest Marke', *Guardian*, 16 September 1995, p.30.

19 Ernest Marke, interview with Michael Butscher, *The Voice*, 20 December 1994, pp.21–22.

20 Learie Constantine, cricketer and politician, was born in 1901 in Petit Valley, Diego Martin, Trinidad.

21 Learie Constantine interviewed by the South African writer Lewis Nkosi in the BBC television documentary *Calypso for Constantine*, shown on BBC1 on 16 June 1966, produced and directed by Malcolm Brown.

22 Ibid.

23 Ibid.

24 Gerald Howat, *Learie Constantine* (George Allen and Unwin, 1975), p.129.

25 *Calypso for Constantine*.

26 Howat, p.29.

27 Peter Mason, *Learie Constantine* (Signal Books, 2008), pp.78–79.

28 Learie Constantine, *Colour Bar* (Stanley Paul, 1954), pp.147–48.

29 Peter Mason, *Learie Constantine*, p.80.

30 Ibid., pp.81, 83.

31 Memo from G.R. Barnes, director of talks, to Miss Bucknall, 8 July 1943 in BBC Written Archives.

32 David Killingray, 'Sir Learie Constantine', *The Oxford Companion to Black British History* (Oxford University Press, 2007), pp.114–16.

33 Law reports in *The Times*, 20 June, 22 June and 29 June 1944.

34 *News Letter*, 58 (July 1944), p.66.

35 *Calypso for Constantine*.

36 In the New Year's Honours List for 1946 Constantine was appointed Member of the British Empire (MBE). He appreciated this honour, but took even greater pride in the illuminated scroll he had received from the West Indians he had helped in Liverpool. Qualifying as a barrister, he was called to the Bar in 1954. In 1947, following the death of Dr Harold Moody, he briefly became president of the League of Coloured Peoples. In 1961 he became Trinidad and Tobago's first high commissioner to London. A knighthood followed in 1962, and in 1969 he became a peer and the first black member of the House of Lords.

Chapter 3

1 *Wonderful Adventures of Mrs Seacole in many lands* was reprinted by Falling Wall Press in 1984 with a new introduction by Ziggi Alexander and Audrey Dewjee.

2 While Britain's black community has given her prominence (for example, in 2004 she was voted number one in Patrick Vernon's *100 Great Black Britons* poll on the *Everygeneration* website), in the mainstream Seacole tends to stand

alone as a black British female historical figure in published works. Among the exceptions are several reprints – from 1993 – of *The History of Mary Prince, a West Indian Slave* (1831) and *The Oxford Companion to Black British History*, published by the Oxford University Press in 2007 which, in addition to Mary Seacole, includes a number of biographical entries for black British women.

3 Delia Jarrett-Macauley, 'Putting the Black Woman in the Frame: Una Marson and the West Indian Challenge to the British National Identity', in Christine Gledhill and Gillian Swanson (eds), *Nationalising Femininity: Culture, Sexuality and British Cinema in the Second World War* (Manchester University Press, 1996), p.117.

4 Ben Bousquet and Colin Douglas, *West Indian Women at War – British Racism in World War II* (Lawrence and Wishart, 1991), p.ix.

5 Letter from Mrs Uroom to Winston Churchill, 10 October 1941, PRO CO 859 77/1.

6 Ibid.

7 Peter Fryer, *Staying Power – The History of Black People in Britain* (Pluto Press, 1984), p.364; *Parliamentary Debates*, 5th series, vol. 392 (1943), cols. 390–1.

8 Graham A. Smith, 'Jim Crow on the Home Front (1942–1945)', *New Community*, Winter 1980, vol. 3, p.325.

9 Angelina Osborne and Arthur Torrington, *We Served – The Untold Story of the West Indian Contribution to World War II* (Krik Krak Publishing, 2005).

10 Ben Bousquet, *The Forgotten Volunteers*, BBC Radio 2, 11 November 2000.

11 Norma Best, *Forgotten Volunteers*.

12 Private information.

13 Ibid.

14 Ibid.

15 Charity Adams Earley, *One Woman's Army – A Black Officer Remembers the WAC* (Texas A&M University Press, 1989), p.135.

16 Ibid., p.138.

17 *The Birmingham Post*, 14 February 1945, p.1.

18 *The Birmingham Sunday Mercury*, 13 February 1945, p.11. In 1981 nine members of the 6888th postal unit took a nostalgic trip back to Birmingham. It was the first time they had been back to the city since 1945. The women were met by the lord mayor and visited the old Birmingham school house where they had been billeted for about five months. See 'Tripping Down Memory Lane', *Evening Mail*, 29 April 1981, p.7.

19 Kenneth Trotman interviewed in Colin Prescod's documentary *Tiger Bay is My Home* (1984), made for the Channel 4 television series *Struggles for Black Community*. Trotman died in Cardiff in 1999 at the age of 93.

20 Neil M.C. Sinclair, *The Tiger Bay Story* (Butetown History and Arts Project, 1993), p.26.

21 For further information about Butetown and the Second World War see Alan Llwyd, *Cymru Ddu – Hanes Pobl Dduon Cymru / Black Wales – A History of Black Welsh People* (Hughes/Butetown History and Arts Centre, 2005). Also, 'Butetown Remembers World War II – Seamen, the Forces, Evacuees', an exhibition by the Butetown History and Arts Centre presented in 2005.

22 Grace Wilkie was interviewed in *The Mother Country*, part one of the television series *Black Britain* shown on BBC2 on 7 January 1991. See also Ray Costello, *Black Liverpool – The Early History of Britain's Oldest Black Community 1730–1918* (Picton Press, 2001). For information about Derry Wilkie, see Ray Costello, *Liverpool's Black Pioneers* (The Bluecoat Press, 2007), pp.124–126.

23 Lilian Bailey was born at 19 Stanhope Street, Toxteth Park, Liverpool, in 1918. Her life story is told in the booklet *Together – Lilian Bader: Wartime Memoirs of a WAAF 1939–1944*, published by the Imperial War Museum from an interview recorded in 1989 with Lilian and the Imperial War Museum's sound archive.

24 Bousquet and Douglas, p.17.

25 Private information.

26 Bader, *Together*, p.2.

27 Lilian Bader, *Forgotten Volunteers*.

28 Bader, *Together*, p.5.

29 Ray Costello, *Black Liverpool*, pp.53–54.

30 Bader, *Together*, p.9.

31 Ibid., pp.11–12.

32 Bader, *Forgotten Volunteers*.

33 Bousquet and Douglas, pp.76–77.

34 Jacqueline Harriott, *Black Women in Britain* (B.T. Batsford, 1992), p.42.

35 Pauline Henriques was born in Half Way Tree, Kingston, Jamaica, in 1914 and died in 1998 at the age of 84. The Henriques family arrived in Liverpool from Kingston on 4 May 1919. Pauline's experiences of the Second World War have been documented by Mavis Nicholson in *What Did You Do in the War, Mummy?* (Chatto and Windus, 1995).

36 Pauline Henriques, interview with Stephen Bourne, Brighton, 4 August 1989.

37 Pauline Crabbe, 'Cutting the Apron Strings', Mavis Nicholson, *What Did You Do in the War, Mummy?* (Chatto and Windus, 1995), p.23.

38 Ibid., pp.23–24.

39 Ibid., p.24.

40 Pauline Henriques, interview with Stephen Bourne, Brighton, 8 March 1995.

41 Nicholson, p.27.

42 Jenni Murray, *The Woman's Hour – 50 Years of Women in Britain* (BBC Books, 1996), p.69.

43 Ibid.

44 Henriques, interview with Stephen Bourne, 8 March 1995.

45 Nicholson, p.30.

Chapter 4

1 Josephine Esther Bruce was born in Fulham in 1912 and died in 1994 at the age of 81. Her life story was told in *Aunt Esther's Story*, co-authored with her adopted nephew Stephen Bourne. It was published in 1991 by Hammersmith and Fulham's Ethnic Communities Oral History Project and received the Raymond Williams Prize for Community Publishing. A revised, updated edition was published in 1996. In 2007 Stephen Bourne and Andrew

Warrington co-produced a short documentary about Esther Bruce, also called *Aunt Esther's Story*.

2 Stephen Bourne, 'Esther Bruce' in *Oxford Dictionary of National Biography* (Oxford University Press, 2004) and 'Esther Bruce' in *The Oxford Companion to Black British History* (Oxford University Press, 2007), p.74.

3 Stephen Bourne and Esther Bruce, *Aunt Esther's Story* (Hammersmith and Fulham Ethnic Communities Oral History Project, 2nd edition, 1996), p.14.

4 Colin Grant, *Negro With a Hat* (Jonathan Cape, 2008).

5 Bourne and Bruce, p.7.

6 Private information.

7 Ibid.

8 Ibid.

9 Bourne and Bruce, p.11.

10 Private information.

11 Ibid.

12 Bourne and Bruce, p.16.

13 Jack Forth, letter to Stephen Bourne, 30 October 2007.

14 Private information.

15 Bourne and Bruce, p.11.

16 Mavis Nicholson, *What Did You Do in the War, Mummy?* (Chatto and Windus, 1995), p.30.

17 Private information.

18 Leslie Hasker, *Fulham in the Second World War* (Fulham and Hammersmith Historical Society, 1984), p.80.

19 Bourne and Bruce, pp.12–13.

20 Private information.

21 Bourne and Bruce, p.13.

22 Ibid., p.14.

Chapter 5

1 Ben Wicks, *No Time to Wave Goodbye – The Story of Britain's 3,500,000 Evacuees* (Bloomsbury, 1988), p.97.

2 *London Calling*, 20 January 1940, p.4.

3 Ibid.

4 League of Coloured Peoples, Letter No 2, News Notes (November 1939), p.2.

5 Neil M.C. Sinclair, *The Tiger Bay Story* (Butetown History and Arts Project, 1993), p.45.

6 Howard Bloch, 'Black People in Canning Town and Custom House between the Wars', *Association for the Study of African, Caribbean and Asian Culture and History in Britain*, Newsletter 14 (January 1996), p.5.

7 Anita Bowes, interview with Stephen Bourne, London, 27 January 1996.

8 Christopher Cozier, interview with Stephen Bourne, London, 1 March 1996.

9 Joseph Cozier, interview with Stephen Bourne, London, 9 March 1996.

10 Kenny Lynch, interview with Stephen Bourne, London, 24 July 1991. Kenny Lynch entered show business as a dance band singer in the 1950s and rose to

fame in the 1960s as a singer and songwriter. He had a number of recording successes, including *Up on the Roof* in 1962, and subsequently made numerous television appearances. In 1970 Kenny was awarded an OBE for his charity work.

11 Marie Kamara, interviewed by Mel Odusanya, *History Talk*, Community History Newsletter 8 (February 2006), p.4. Also interviewed by Stephen Bourne, London, 9 December 2007.

12 Ibid.

13 Ibid.

14 *Where Were You On the Day War Broke Out?*, written by John Lloyd, produced by Therese Denny, BBC1, 3 September 1969.

Chapter 6

1 Richard Smith, 'Second World War', *The Oxford Companion to Black British History* (Oxford University Press, 2007), p.436.

2 'West Indian Craftsmen for Britain', League of Coloured Peoples, *News Letter*, 18 (March 1941), p.132.

3 *News Letter*, 26 (November 1941), pp.28–30.

4 *News Letter*, 34 (July 1942), pp.87–88.

5 Graham Smith, 'Jim Crow on the home front (1942–1945)', *New Community*, III/33 (Winter 1980), pp.17–28.

6 Liverpool-born Dame Rose Heilbron QC was an outstanding defence barrister whose career included many 'firsts' for a woman: she was the first woman to win a scholarship to Gray's Inn; the first woman to be appointed King's Counsel; the first to lead in a murder case; the first woman Recorder; the first woman judge to sit at the Old Bailey; and the first woman treasurer at Gray's Inn. Heilbron was junior counsel in some notable reported cases of the 1940s, including *Constantine* v. *Imperial Hotels Ltd* (1944) (see Chapter 2).

7 Carlton Wilson, 'Liverpool's Black Population During World War II', *Black and Asian Studies Newsletter*, 20 (January 1998), pp.14–15.

8 *Guardian*, 2 August 1944 and *News Letter*, 60 (September 1944), pp.93–94.

9 *News Letter*, 71 (August 1945), p.108.

10 'The Cardiff Coloured Mission', *News Letter*, 29 (February 1942), p.110.

11 *News Letter*, 55 (April 1944), pp.5–6.

12 Kenneth Little, *Negroes in Britain – A Study of Racial Relations in English Society* (Kegan Paul, 1948), pp.116–17.

13 Ibid.

14 A.L. Lloyd, *Picture Post*, Vol. 47, No 4 (22 April 1950), pp.13–19.

15 *News Letter*, 11 (August 1940), pp.86–87.

16 Letter from Sapper Box's commanding officer to *News Letter*, 13 (October 1940), p.14.

17 A.A. Thompson, 'Coloured People and the London Blitz', *News Letter*, 15 (December 1940), pp.67–68.

18 Further investigation reveals that Stafford 'Buzz' Barton was a middleweight boxing champion who was active in the 1930s. He claimed to be 19 years

old in 1934, was the son of the news editor for Jamaica's *Daily Gleaner* and joined London's Air Raid Precautions as early as September 1939 (source: *The Illustrated Sporting and Dramatic News*, 22 September 1939). The website of the Commonwealth War Graves Commission (www.cwgc.com) confirms that, as a member of the RAF Volunteer Reserve, Sergeant Stafford Alfonzo Barton of 142 Squadron was killed in action in the Mediterranean on 24 November 1943. He is buried in Staglieno cemetery in Genoa.

19 Fernando Henriques, *Children of Caliban – Miscegenation* (Secker and Warburg, 1974), p.3.

20 Ibid.

21 Ibid.

22 Fernando Henriques, 'Coloured Men in Civilian Defence', *News Letter*, 21 (June 1941), pp.57–59.

23 Oku Ekpenyon, 'An ARP Man's Story', *BBC History Magazine*, 1/5 (September 2000), p.47.

24 E.I. Ekpenyon, *Some Experiences of an African Air-Raid Warden* (The Sheldon Press, 1943), p.10.

25 *Calling West Africa*, a talk by E.I. Ekpenyon, 11 July 1941, script in BBC Written Archives.

26 Ekpenyon, *Some Experiences of an African Air-Raid Warden*, pp.7–8.

27 *Calling West Africa*, presentation of Katsina by E.I. Ekpenyon, 18 July 1942, script in BBC Written Archives.

28 Leonard Bradbrook was born in 1904 in Fitzalan Street. His mother Amy was a charwoman. The name of his father was not recorded on his birth certificate. Thanks to Gabrielle Bourn, the learning development officer for Lambeth Archives, for sharing this information with me.

29 Len Bradbrook interviewed in *A Century of Childhood* (Sidgwick and Jackson, 1988), p.129.

30 Daisy Moore in Allen Eyles and Margaret O'Brien (eds), *Enter the Dream-House: Memoirs of Cinemas in South London from the Twenties to the Sixties* (British Film Institute, 1993), p.51.

31 For further information about Len see Michael Herbert, *Never Counted Out! The Story of Len Johnson, Manchester's Black Boxing Hero and Communist* (Dropped Aitches Press, 1992) and Rob Howard, *Boxing's Uncrowned Champion – Len Johnson and the Colour Bar* (Rob Howard, 2009).

32 Herbert, *Never Counted Out!*, p.64. Thanks to Michael Herbert for sharing his correspondence about Len Johnson's wartime experiences.

Chapter 7

1 Letter from Mrs Florence Cross to Stephen Bourne, 10 June 2000.

2 Adelaide Hall was born in Brooklyn, New York, in 1901. She died in London in 1993.

3 Iain Cameron Williams, *Underneath a Harlem Moon – The Harlem to Paris Years of Adelaide Hall* (Continuum, 2002) and Stephen Bourne, 'The Real First Lady of Jazz', *Guardian*, 25 January 2003, p.16.

4 Olufela 'Fela' Sowande was born in Oyo, Nigeria, in 1905. He died in 1987. See Stephen Bourne, 'Fela for the Rhythm', *The Stage*, 29 July 2004, p.19.

5 Stephen Bourne, *Sophisticated Lady – A Celebration of Adelaide Hall* (ECOHP, 2001), p.43.

6 Ibid., p.44.

7 *The Stage*, 'Raids and Entertainments', 29 August 1940, p.2.

8 *The Kentish Mercury*, 'In Cinemas and Theatres', 30 August 1940, p.1.

9 Bourne, *Sophisticated Lady*, p.44.

10 Ibid., pp.43–44.

11 Incident No 683 in the City of Westminster Civil Defence Records held in the City of Westminster Archives Centre.

12 Bourne, *Sophisticated Lady*, p.45.

13 Ibid.

14 Letter to Stephen Bourne from Geoffrey Noble, English Heritage Blue Plaques Secretary, 25 April 2002. Adelaide deserves better, although she has been acknowledged in three important exhibitions about the Second World War: the Imperial War Museum's 'Women and War' (2003) and 'Outbreak 1939' (2009); and the Cuming Museum's 'Keep Smiling Through – Black Londoners on the Home Front 1939–1945' (2008).

Chapter 8

1 Charlotte Breese, *Hutch* (Bloomsbury, 1999), pp.182–83.

2 Leslie Hutchinson was born on the Caribbean island of Grenada in 1900. He was of mixed African, Caribbean, Indian, Scottish and French ancestry.

3 Elisabeth Welch, interview with Stephen Bourne, London, 15 August 1993.

4 Charlotte Breese and Hugh Bredin, *Hutch – Magic Abroad and in the Air*, compact disc sleeve notes (Holland, 1999).

5 Charlotte Breese interviewed by Stephen Bourne in *Salutations*, BBC Radio 2, 11 September 1993.

6 Adelaide Hall, interview with Stephen Bourne, London, 21 July 1993.

7 Breese, *Hutch*, p.165.

8 *The Stage*, 19 March 1942, p.19.

9 Breese, *Hutch*, p.165.

10 Contrary to popular belief, Hutch has not been forgotten. Since his death, in addition to Charlotte Breese's biography, there have been many reissues of his vast recording output on long-playing records and compact discs, as well as five profiles on BBC Radio 2: *Old Stagers* (1984), *Salutations* (1993) presented by Moira Stuart, *The Sexton's Tales* (1997), *The Torch Singers* (2002) presented by Eartha Kitt, and *Desmond Carrington* (2005). In 2004 Hutch was heard singing on the soundtrack of the BBC2 television documentary *Dunkirk – The Soldier's Story*, and in 2008 Channel 4 screened a television documentary about Hutch called *High Society's Favourite Gigolo*.

11 Elisabeth Welch was born in New York in 1904. She died in London in 2003. For further information see Stephen Bourne, *Elisabeth Welch – Soft Lights and Sweet Music* (Scarecrow Press, 2005).

12 Richard Fawkes, *Fighting for a Laugh – Entertaining the British and American Armed Forces 1939–1946* (Macdonald and Jane's, 1978), p.19.

13 Private information.

14 Elisabeth Welch, 'A Night to Remember', *Sunday Telegraph*, 29 November 1992, p.18.

15 Ibid.

16 Kenrick Hijmans Johnson was born in Georgetown, British Guiana, in 1914.

17 For further information about Buddy Bradley see Stephen Bourne, 'Harlem Comes to London', *Black in the British Frame – The Black Experience in British Film and Television* (Continuum, 2001).

18 Leslie Thompson and Jeffrey P. Green, *Leslie Thompson – An Autobiography* (Rabbit Press, 1985), pp.89–105.

19 Bourne, *Soft Lights and Sweet Music*, p.36.

20 Elaine Delmar, interview with Stephen Bourne, London, 16 August, 1993.

21 Charles Graves, *Champagne and Chandeliers – The Story of the Café de Paris* (Odhams Press, 1958), p.112.

22 Ibid., p.117.

23 Joe Deniz, interview with Stephen Bourne, London, 10 August 1993.

24 Val Wilmer, 'First Sultan of Swing', *The Independent on Sunday*, 24 February 1991, p.10.

25 Graves, pp.118–19.

26 Philip Ziegler, *London at War 1939–1945* (Sinclair-Stevenson, 1995), p.148.

27 Angus Calder, *The People's War* (Jonathan Cape, 1969), p.204.

28 For further information about Ken 'Snakehips' Johnson see Andrew Simons, *Black British Swing*, compact disc sleeve notes (Topic/National Sound Archive, 2001) and Andrew Winton's *Swingtime* website: www.swingtime. co.uk.

Chapter 9

1 Elisabeth Welch interviewed by Stephen Bourne in Jim Pines (ed.), *Black and White in Colour – Black People in British Television Since 1936* (British Film Institute, 1992), p.24.

2 Evelyn Dove was born in London in 1902. She died in 1987. For further information see Stephen Bourne, 'Evelyn Dove', *Oxford Dictionary of National Biography*.

3 Edric Connor was born in Trinidad in 1913. He died in 1968. For further information see Stephen Bourne, 'A Man For All Seasons' in *Black in the British Frame – The Black Experience in British Film and Television* (Continuum, 2001) and 'Edric Connor', *Oxford Dictionary of National Biography*.

4 Edric Connor, *Horizons – The Life and Times of Edric Connor* (Ian Randle, 2007), pp.62–63.

5 Ibid., p.64.

6 Pearl Connor Mogotsi, interviewed by Stephen Bourne, London, 26 July 1993.

7 D.G. Bridson, *Prospero and Ariel – The Rise and Fall of Radio: A Personal Recollection* (Victor Gollancz, 1971), pp.109–11.

8 Una Marson was born in Jamaica in 1905. She died in 1965. For further information see Delia Jarrett-Macauley, *The Life of Una Marson 1905–1965* (Manchester University Press, 1998) and Alison Donnell, 'Una Marson: feminism, anti-colonialism and a forgotten fight for freedom' in Bill Schwarz (ed.), *West Indian Intellectuals in Britain* (Manchester University Press, 2003).

9 Delia Jarrett-Macauley in *Voice – The Una Marson Story*, BBC Radio 3, 23 July 2003.

10 Delia Jarrett-Macauley, *The Life of Una Marson*, p.147.

11 'Una Marson joins the BBC staff', *London Calling*, No 80, 13–19 April 1941, p.13.

12 'Extended service for the West Indies', *London Calling*, No 81, 20–26 April 1941, p.13.

13 Erika Smilowitz, 'Una Marson: Woman Before her Time', *Jamaica Journal*, Vol. 16, No 2, May 1983, pp.62–68.

14 Delia Jarrett-Macauley, interviewed by Jane Garvey, *Woman's Hour*, BBC Radio 4, 3 March 2009.

15 For further information about *Caribbean Voices* see Glyne Griffith, 'This is London Calling the West Indies: the BBC's *Caribbean Voices*' in Bill Schwarz (ed.), *West Indian Intellectuals in Britain* (Manchester University Press, 2003).

16 *The Life of Una Marson*, p.160.

17 *News Letter*, 67 (April 1945), p.8.

18 In 1948 Kenneth Little published one of the earliest studies of black people in Britain called *Negroes in Britain – A Study in Racial Relations in English Society* (Kegan Paul).

19 For further information see Memo from BBC Liaison Officer Mrs Elspeth Huxley to Director of Talks G.R. Barnes, 'Colour Prejudice Discussion', 25 June 1943, and Memo from G.R. Barnes to Miss Bucknall, 'Discussion on Colour Prejudice', 30 June 1943, BBC Written Archives.

Chapter 10

1 Monolulu was born Peter McKay in British Guiana in 1881. He arrived in Britain in 1902 and died in London in 1965 at the age of 84. On his death certificate his occupation is entered as 'Racehorse Betting Adviser'.

2 Marie Seton, *Paul Robeson* (Dennis Dobson, 1958), p.78.

3 Paul Robeson Jr, *The Undiscovered Paul Robeson – An Artist's Journey, 1898–1939* (John Wiley & Sons, 2001), pp.330–31.

4 Peter Noble, *The Negro in Films* (Skelton Robinson, 1948), p.127.

5 James Walvin, *Black and White – The Negro and English Society 1555–1945* (Allen Lane/The Penguin Press, 1973), p.213.

6 Graham Smith, *When Jim Crow Met John Bull – Black American Soldiers in World War II Britain* (I.B. Tauris, 1987), p.88.

7 Ibid., pp.88–89.

8 *West Indies Calling* is a shorter version of *Hello! West Indies*, which was distributed in the West Indies.

9 After appearing in *West Indies Calling*, Squadron Leader Ulric Cross was awarded the Distinguished Flying Cross (DFC) in 1944 for his gallantry during

the Second World War. While serving as a pilot officer with 139 (Jamaica) Squadron, he participated in bombing attacks across occupied Europe. In 1945 he was also awarded the Distinguished Service Order (DSO) in recognition of his 'fine example of keenness and devotion to duty' and 'exceptional navigational ability'.

10 Wendy Webster, *Englishness and Empire 1939–1965* (Oxford University Press, 2005), p.41.

11 Ibid., p.42.

12 George Pearson, *Flashback – The Autobiography of a Film-Maker* (George Allen and Unwin, 1957), p.204.

13 *Colonial Cinema*, 1944, 2, 1, p.3.

14 'African Princess As Nurse', *The British Journal of Nursing*, January 1938, p.16.

15 League of Coloured Peoples, *News Letter*, 65 (February 1945), p.102. For further information about the CFU and Africa see Rosaleen Smyth, 'The British Colonial Film Unit and Sub-Saharan Africa, 1939–1945', *Historical Journal of Film, Radio and Television*, Vol. 8, No 3 (1988), pp.285–98.

16 Catherine Collins, 'Stephanie's crown was a first – and captured on film', *Northants Evening Telegraph*, 1 September 2009. See also Vanessa Thorpe, 'Propaganda coup of England's first black May Queen', *The Observer*, 21 June 2009.

Chapter 11

1 Oliver Marshall, *The Caribbean at War – British West Indians in World War II* (The North Kensington Archive, 1992), p.3. See also Stephen Bourne and Sav Kyriacou, *A Ship and a Prayer* (ECOHP, 1999), p.21. Randolph Beresford was born in Guyana in 1914 and came to Britain in 1953. He became Mayor of Hammersmith and Fulham in 1975 and received the British Empire Medal in 1979 for his community work. He was made an MBE in 1986. Randolph died at the age of 91 in 2005.

2 For further information see Mike Phillips and Trevor Phillips, *Windrush – The Irresistible Rise of Multi-Racial Britain* (HarperCollins, 1998).

3 Constance MacDonald was born in Kingston in 1923. She served in the Auxiliary Territorial Service (ATS) in Jamaica. Connie was awarded the War Medal for her services to the British war effort. In 1954 she left Jamaica and settled in London. She was awarded the British Empire Medal for her services to the community in 1992. Connie died in 2007.

4 Bourne and Kyriacou, p.23.

5 Stephen Bourne, *Speak of me as I am – The Black Presence in Southwark Since 1600* (Southwark Council, 2005), p.64. Sam King was born in Jamaica in 1926. After his war service in the RAF, Sam returned to Britain on the Empire Windrush in 1948. He became the first black Mayor of Southwark in 1983 and for his services to the community he received an MBE in 1998.

6 Austin Clarke, *Growing Up Stupid Under the Union Jack – A Memoir* (Ian Randle Publishers, 2003), p.49.

7 See Olive R. Cruchley, 'Visit to British Honduras Camp in Scotland' in League of Coloured Peoples, *News Letter*, 27 (December 1941) and Amos A. Ford,

Telling the Truth – The Life and Times of the British Honduran Forestry Unit in Scotland (1941–44) (Karia Press, 1985).

8 See CD compilation *West Indian Rhythm – Trinidad Calypsos on world and local events featuring the censored recordings, 1938–1940*.

9 Bourne and Kyriacou, p.23.

10 Norman Beaton, *Beaton But Unbowed – An Autobiography* (Methuen, 1986), p.35.

11 Clarke, pp.95–96.

12 Dr Harold Moody, League of Coloured Peoples, *News Letter*, 12 (September 1940).

13 *News Letter*, 14 (November 1940), p.33.

Postscript

1 'The Forgotten Black Victims of Nazi Germany – What Hitler did to the races he deemed "inferior"', *The Voice* (16–22 February 2009), pp.16–17.

2 May Opitz, Katharina Oguntoye and Dagmar Schultz (eds), *Showing Our Colours – Afro-German Women Speak Out* (Open Letters, 1992), pp.56–76.

3 John Welch, 'Twelve Years Under Hitler', *Pittsburgh Courier* (1944). No further details available.

4 Adolf Hitler quoted in Roi Ottley, *No Green Pastures* (Charles Scribner's Sons, 1951), p.161.

5 Marie Seton, *Paul Robeson* (Dennis Dobson, 1958), p.83.

6 Wikipedia and Jonathan Croall, *Sybil Thorndike – A Star for Life* (Haus Books, 2008), p.356.

7 Norman Longmate, letter to Stephen Bourne, 23 February 2006.

8 *Here-Say*, BBC2, tx 7 August 1990.

FURTHER READING

Adams Earley, Charity (1989), *One Woman's Army – A Black Officer Remembers the WAC*, Texas A & M University Press.

Adi, Hakim (1995), *The History of the African and Caribbean Communities in Britain*, Wayland.

———— (1998), *West Africans in Britain 1900–1960: Nationalism, Pan-Africanism and Communism*, Lawence and Wishart.

Adi, Hakim and Sherwood, Marika (1995), *The 1945 Manchester Pan-African Congress Revisited*, New Beacon Books.

Anim-Addo, Joan (1995), *Longest Journey – A History of Black Lewisham*, Deptford Forum Publishing.

Bourne, Stephen (September 2000), 'We Also Served – Black Britons on the Home Front', *BBC History Magazine*, 1/5, pp.46–48.

———— (2001), *Black in the British Frame – The Black Experience in British Film and Television* (2nd edition), Continuum.

———— (2001), *Sophisticated Lady – A Celebration of Adelaide Hall*, ECOHP.

———— (January 2003), 'We Also Served', *Black and Asian Studies Association Newsletter* 35, pp.12–15.

———— (2005), *Elisabeth Welch – Soft Lights and Sweet Music*, Scarecrow Press.

———— (2005), *Speak of Me As I Am – The Black Presence in Southwark Since 1600*, Southwark Council.

———— (2008), *Dr Harold Moody*, Southwark Council.

Bourne, Stephen and Bruce, Esther (1996), *Aunt Esther's Story* (2nd edition), ECOHP.

Bourne, Stephen and Kyriacou, Sav (1999), *A Ship and a Prayer – The Black Presence in Hammersmith and Fulham*, ECOHP.

Bousquet, Ben and Douglas, Colin (1991), *West Indian Women at War – British Racism in World War II*, Lawrence and Wishart.

Breese, Charlotte (1999), *Hutch*, Bloomsbury.

Bridson, D.G. (1971), *Prospero and Ariel – The Rise and Fall of Radio: A Personal Recollection*, Victor Gollancz.

Calder, Angus (1969), *The People's War*, Jonathan Cape.

Cameron Williams, Iain (2002), *Underneath a Harlem Moon – The Harlem to Paris Years of Adelaide Hall*, Continuum.

Clarke, Austin (2003), *Growing Up Stupid Under the Union Jack – A Memoir*, Ian Randle.

Clarke, Peter B. (1986), *West Africans at War 1918–1914 and 1939–1945*, Ethnographica.

Connor, Edric (2007), *Horizons – The Life and Times of Edric Connor 1913–1968: An Autobiography*, Ian Randle.

Constantine, Learie (1954), *Colour Bar*, Stanley Paul.

Costello, Ray (2001), *Black Liverpool – The Early History of Britain's Oldest Black Community 1730–1918*, Picton Press (Liverpool).

Dabydeen, David, Gilmore, John and Jones, Cecily (eds) (2007), *The Oxford Companion to Black British History*, Oxford University Press.

Ethnic Communities Oral History Project (1989), *The Motherland Calls – African Caribbean Experiences*, Hammersmith and Fulham Community History Series No 4/ECOHP.

Fawkes, Richard (1978), *Fighting for a Laugh – Entertaining the British and American Armed Forces 1939–1946*, Macdonald and Jane's.

File, Nigel and Power, Chris (1981), *Black Settlers in Britain 1555–1958*, Heinemann.

Ford, Amos A. (1985), *Telling the Truth – The Life and Times of the British Honduran Forestry Unit in Scotland (1941–44)*, Karia Press.

Fryer, Peter (1984), *Staying Power – The History of Black People in Britain*, Pluto.

Gardiner, Juliet (2004), *Wartime Britain 1939–1945*, Headline.

Gilroy, Paul (2007), *Black Britain – A Photographic History*, Saqi/Getty Images.

Giuseppi, Undine (1974), *A Look at Learie Constantine*, Thomas Nelson.

Grant, Cy (2006), *'A Member of the RAF of Indeterminate Race' – WW2 experiences of a former RAF Navigator and POW*, Woodfield Publishing.

———— (2007), *Blackness and the Dreaming Soul*, Shoving Leopard.

Graves, Charles (1958), *Champagne and Chandeliers – The Story of the Café de Paris*, Odhams Press.

Haining, Peter (1989), *The Day War Broke Out – 3 September 1939*, W.H. Allen.

Harriott, Jacqueline (1992), *Black Women in Britain (Women Making History* series), B.T. Batsford.

Havers, Richard (2007), *Here is the News – The BBC and the Second World War*, Sutton Publishing.

Henfrey, June and Law, Ian (1981), *A History of Race and Racism in Liverpool, 1660–1950*, Merseyside Community Relations Council.

Henriques, Fernando (1974), *Children of Caliban – Miscegenation*, Secker and Warburg.

Herbert, Michael (1992), *Never Counted Out! The Story of Len Johnson, Manchester's Black Boxing Hero and Communist*, Dropped Aitches Press.

Hickman, Tom (1995), *What did you do in the War, Auntie? – The BBC at War 1939–45*, BBC Books.

Howard, Rob (2009), *Boxing's Uncrowned Champion – Len Johnson and the Colour Bar*, Rob Howard.

Howat, Gerald (1975), *Learie Constantine*, George Allen.

Further Reading

Imperial War Museum (1995), 'Together' – a multi-media resource pack on the contribution made in the Second World War by African, Asian and Caribbean men and women.

Jarrett-Macauley, Delia (1998), *The Life of Una Marson 1905–65*, Manchester University Press.

Killingray, David and Rathbone, Richard (1986), *Africa and the Second World War*, Macmillan.

King, Sam (1998), *Climbing Up the Rough Side of the Mountain*, Minerva Press.

Lewis, Peter (1986), *The People's War*, Thames Methuen.

Little, Kenneth (1948), *Negroes in Britain – A Study in Racial Relations in English Society*, Kegan Paul.

Lotz, Rainer and Pegg, Ian (1986), *Under the Imperial Carpet – Essays in Black History 1780–1950*, Rabbit Press.

Lusane, Clarence (2002), *Hitler's Black Victims – The Historical Experiences of Afro-Germans, European Blacks, Africans, and African Americans in the Nazi Era*, Routledge.

McGuire, Phillip (ed.) (1983), *Taps for a Jim Crow Army – Black Soldiers in World War II*, University Press of Kentucky.

McKenzie-Mavinga, Isha and Perkins, Thelma (1991), *In Search of Mr McKenzie – Two Sisters' Quest for an Unknown Father*, The Women's Press.

Marke, Ernest (1975), *Old Man Trouble*, Weidenfeld and Nicolson.

Marshall, Oliver (1992), *The Caribbean at War – British West Indians in World War II*, North Kensington Archive.

Mason, Peter (2008), *Caribbean Lives – Learie Constantine*, Signal Books.

Massaquoi, Hans J. (2001), *Destined to Witness – Growing Up Black in Nazi Germany*, Fusion Press.

Miller, Mark (2007), *High Hat, Trumpet and Rhythm – The Life and Music of Valaida Snow*, The Mercury Press.

Monolulu, Ras Prince (1950), *I Gotta Horse – The Autobiography of Ras Prince Monolulu*, Hurst and Blackett.

Moore, Brenda L. (1996), *To Serve My Country, To Serve My Race – The Story of the Only African American WACs Stationed Overseas During World War II*, New York University Press.

Murray, Robert N. (1996), *Lest We Forget – The Experiences of World War II West Indian Ex-Service Personnel*, Nottingham West Indian Combined Ex-Services Association/Hansib.

Nicholson, Mavis (1995), *What Did You Do in the War, Mummy?* Chatto and Windus.

Noble, E. Martin (1984), *Jamaica Airman – A Black Airman in Britain 1943 and After*, New Beacon Books.

Notting Dale Urban Studies Centre and Ethnic Communities Oral History Project (1992), *Sorry No Vacancies – Life Stories of Senior Citizens from the Caribbean*, Notting Dale Urban Studies Centre/ECOHP.

Oliver, Paul (ed.) (1990), *Black Music in Britain – Essays on the Afro-Asian Contribution to Popular Music*, Open University Press.

Opitz, May, Oguntoye, Katharina and Schultz, Dagmar (1992), *Showing Our Colours – Afro-German Women Speak Out*, Open Letters.

Osborne, Angelina and Torrington, Arthur (2005), *We Served – The Untold Story of the West Indian Contribution to World War II*, Krik Krak.

Penick Motley, Mary (1987), *The Invisible Soldier – The Experience of the Black Soldier, World War II*, Wayne State University Press.

Phillips, Mike and Phillips, Trevor (1998), *Windrush – The Irresistible Rise of Multi-Racial Britain*, HarperCollins.

Sandhu, Sukhdev (2003), *London Calling – How Black and Asian Writers Imagined a City*, HarperCollins.

Schwarz, Bill (ed.) (2003), *West Indian Intellectuals in Britain*, Manchester University Press.

Scobie, Edward (1972), *Black Britannia – A History of Blacks in Britain*, Johnson Publishing Company.

Shepherd, Verene A. (1989), *Women in Caribbean History*, Ian Randle.

Sherwood, Marika (1985), *Many Struggles – West Indian Workers and Service Personnel in Britain (1939–1945)*, Karia Press.

———— (1994), *Pastor Daniels Ekarte and the African Churches Mission*, The Savannah Press.

Sherwood, Marika and Spafford, Martin (1999), *Whose Freedom Were Africans, Caribbeans and Indians Fighting for in World War II?* The Savannah Press/Black and Asian Studies Association (pack for schools).

Sinclair, Neil M.C. (1993), *The Tiger Bay Story*, Butetown History and Arts Project.

Smith, Graham (Winter 1980), 'Jim Crow on the home front (1942–1945)', *New Community*, III/33, pp.17–28.

———— (1987), *When Jim Crow Met John Bull – Black American Soldiers in World War II Britain*, I.B. Tauris.

Smith, Stephen D. (1998), *Charlie – The Charlie Williams Story*, Neville-Douglas.

Thompson, Leslie (1985), *Leslie Thompson – An Autobiography* (as told to Jeffrey P. Green), Rabbit Press.

Turpin, Jackie and Fox, W. Terry (2005), *Battling Jack – You Gotta Fight Back*, Mainstream Publishing.

Vaughan, David A. (1950), *Negro Victory – The Life Story of Dr Harold Moody*, Independent Press.

Walker, Sam and Elcock, Alvin (eds) (1998), *The Windrush Legacy – Memories of Britains's post-war Caribbean Immigrants*, The Black Cultural Archives.

Watson, David (1996), 'Black Workers in London in the 1940s', *Historical Studies in Industrial Relations*, No 1, pp.149–58.

Webster, Wendy (2005), *Englishness and Empire 1939–1965*, Oxford University Press.

Wilson, Carlton (January 1998), 'Liverpool's Black Population during World War II', *Black and Asian Studies Association Newsletter*, 20, pp.6–18.

Wood, Jonathan (2006), *Bill Miller – Black Labour Party Activist in Plymouth*, History and Social Action Publications for Labour Heritage.

Yass, Marion (1971), *The Home Front – England 1939–1945*, Wayland.

Ziegler, Philip (1995), *London at War 1939–1945*, Sinclair-Stevenson.

ABOUT THE AUTHOR

Stephen Bourne grew up on a council estate in Peckham, south-east London, and left school in 1974 at the age of 16 with no qualifications. He describes his research methods as self-taught, but in spite of his educationally disadvantaged background he has two degrees and is an authority on black British history.

From 1989 to 1992 Stephen was employed by the BFI/BBC as a researcher on *Black and White in Colour*, a ground-breaking project that unearthed the history of race and representation on British television.

In 1991 Stephen was one of the founder members of the Black and Asian Studies Association. Also in 1991 he co-authored his first book, *Aunt Esther's Story*, with his adopted aunt, a black seamstress born in London in the Edwardian era.

Stephen is the author of two acclaimed histories of British popular cinema: *Brief Encounters – Lesbians and Gays in British Cinema* (1996) and *Black in the British Frame – The Black Experience in British Film and Television* (2001). In 2008 Stephen researched 'Keep Smiling Through – Black Londoners on the Home Front 1939–1945', an exhibition for the Cuming Museum in Walworth Road, SE17, and was a historical consultant for the Imperial War Museum's 'War to Windrush' exhibition. Stephen is also the author of *A Ship and a Prayer* (1999); *Sophisticated Lady – A Celebration of Adelaide Hall* (2001); *Elisabeth Welch – Soft Lights and Sweet Music* (2005); *Speak of Me As I Am – The Black Presence in Southwark Since 1600* (2005); *Ethel Waters – Stormy Weather* (2007); *Butterfly McQueen Remembered* (2008) and *Dr Harold Moody* (2008). He has also contributed to *The Encyclopaedia of British Film* (2003) and *The Oxford Companion to Black British History* (2007).

Stephen has received two Race in the Media awards from the Commission for Racial Equality, and for *Black in the British Frame* he was short-listed for *The Voice* newspaper's Black Community Award for Literature.

For further information go to www.stephenbourne.co.uk

INDEX

People

Places